Voice Student's

Sing!

Vocal Theory and
Exercise Instructions

Jane Edgren

Voice Student's Edition Sing!
Vocal Theory and Exercise Instructions
Author: Jane Edgren
Copyright © 2019 Vocal Fitness Training, LLC All rights reserved.

First Printing: 2019
ISBN 978-1797966410
Vocal Fitness Training, LLC VocalFitnessStudio.com info@VocalFitnessStudio.com

Included with your purchase of this book is a free 12-month Online Access to Audio Tracks, Instructional Videos and Practice Plans. Coupon code can be found on page 162.

Notice to the Reader

TABLE OF CONTENTS

Horizontal Stretch
Launching Vowel Exercises with the Consonant Sound "y"

HOW THE VOICE WORKS: A VOCAL PRODUCTION PRIMER

Practical Vocal Science
  Reflexive Muscle Memory
The Vocal Cords
The Larynx
The Tongue
Soft Palate
Vocal Tract: The Primary Acoustic Resonator
  Frequencies and Harmonics
  Resonance
  Filtering
Vocal Registers
  Head and Chest Voice?
  Falsetto
  Defining Registers in this Book
Vocal Onset and Stylistic Choices
  Glottal Stop
  Vocal Fry
  Growl
  Rasp or Grit
Contemporary Commercial Music
Pitch
Extending the Vocal Range
In My Studio
The Next Step

THE VOCAL EXERCISE TONE

Practical Vocal Science
  Singing as Elongated Speech
  Vibrato Defined
Practical Exercise Preparation

The Vocal Exercise Tone
Vocal Imagery: A Helpful Tool
In My Studio

HUMMING AND THE /EE/ VOWEL

RESPONSIVE BREATHING

STRENGTHENING THE /EE/ VOWEL

Voiceless Palatal Fricative!
In My Studio
The Next Step

Practical Vocal Science
  Using the Consonant h
  Achieving Vocal Line
  Think Your Way to Legato
How Breathing Technique Enables Vocal Line
Other Helpful Hints
In My Studio

Practical Vocal Science
  The Concept of Vowel Sounds
  Pronunciation Key
  Grouping Vowel Sounds According to Mouth Position
  Smiley Stretch and Pursed Lips
  Using the Natural Smiley Stretch
  Reduced Vowel Sounds' Mouth Positions
Vowel Exercises Using the Natural Smiley Stretch
Exaggeration Is a Tool
In My Studio

VOCAL FITNESS TRAINING EXERCISES AND PRACTICE PLANS

The Practice Room
  Practice Plan 10A
  Practice Plan 10B
Helpful Hints

INTRODUCTION

Welcome to the first book in your journey to improve your singing voice. *Sing! Student Edition* is a course of study that teaches you a solid vocal technique to strengthen and build your voice with simple concepts and terminology through well-constructed vocal exercises.

With your instructor's guidance, this vocal technique will teach you basic healthy, reliable vocal skills for any style of music, with systematic instructions and practicing guidelines from which you can follow a progressive and successful course of study. In addition to the detailed instructions in this book, materials are available through the online audio and video exercises in a self-guided format, free of charge.

Why I Wrote This Vocal Course

When I was young, I took piano lessons using two popular piano methods developed by John Thompson and John W. Schaum respectively, after which I progressed to the standard classical piano repertoire. When my children began piano studies, they too followed a standard teaching method made up of a series of progressive books that taught them the fundamentals. One day it occurred to me that there are very few voice books that offer the same kind of structured and progressive method of teaching basic vocal technique. Therefore, I decided to set out to design and write such a vocal course for students and teachers alike, based on the teaching methods I use in my own studio.

My own singing lessons included study with seven different voice teachers, as well as many vocal coaches. Each one of them brought their own special gifts to the table and helped me to develop my abilities as I gained knowledge and artistry from their teaching. Along the way, experiencing different perspectives and various approaches taught me both how to sing and how not to sing. However, sometimes it was confusing and frustrating to reconcile seemingly conflicting information presented to me as I passed from teacher to teacher, coach to coach.

My teachers always encouraged me to teach voice, and I have done so throughout my singing career. As the years progressed, and as I gained a wealth of experience teaching, I began to refine the way I present information to my students. Many non-classical singers joined my studio with little or no vocal training, and it became very clear to me that their vocal lessons required a new approach. They needed clear and easily understood instruction to give them enough information about the voice without overwhelming them with too much technical detail.

1

Initially, many were concerned that I would teach them a classical technique that would give them a classical sound, but the exercises and approach in this technique are not reflective of any particular singing style (although they certainly are robust enough to develop a classical voice). Rather, following this progressive format of vocal training gives singers a reliable foundation and helps to create sounds that are strong, pure, and healthy.

There are many rewards in teaching voice, but the greatest one is giving singers of all different styles of music a dependable vocal instrument they know how to play. For some, success may come from the joy of singing a solo for the first time in their church. For others, it might be the acquisition of vocal stamina that allows them to tour and sing numerous gigs without constantly losing their voice. Great vocal technique may not guarantee that lucrative recording contract or role on Broadway, but it gives students the tools they need to go wherever their singing takes them.

I had a student come to me who was hoarse every Monday morning after playing weekend gigs with his rock band. He also was having trouble reaching and maintaining his high notes. After studying this vocal technique, he improved to the point where he could sing without any hoarseness and eventually reached the celebrity round of a well-known television singing competition.

Another student came to me after suffering from long-term vocal strain. Once the doctor cleared her to study voice, we worked to change the way she produced her singing tones. She has not had any problems since, and her voice has become stronger as the months have progressed.

My favorite story is that of a student who due to health conditions could no longer continue with her painting career. Needing to feed her artistic side, she decided to join her husband and sing in a local community choir, with no prior singing experience. With a very strong commitment, and hours of practicing, she learned how to sing and over time produced a very pleasant soprano sound.

My desire is to put solid and basic vocal information, instruction, and exercises in the hands of those who would like to improve their voice, no matter what their level of experience. This is more than a curriculum, though, because it integrates your voice teacher's instruction with online audio and video examples that support the exercises. The audio examples include a vocal model indicating how to produce each sound, because learning to sing necessitates aural input, and listening to a proper vocal tone helps to speed up the process.

Even with a voice teacher, singers are ultimately responsible for teaching themselves after they leave their voice lesson. The online components are another part of the learning process, as they provide you with the extra dimension needed to fully understand, implement, and practice the exercises properly and gain the maximum results from this vocal technique. Please use all of the information presented in the written, audio, and video resources to augment, inform, and inspire the vocal study you receive from your teacher.

This first book is just that, a first book. After its completion, I will complete work on modules that will provide further instruction on such subjects as integrating the vocal technique into songs, and intermediate and advanced exercises to develop flexibility and range extension, including strategies and instructions for singing high notes. Each module will indicate whether there is a prerequisite in addition to completing this book, as they will have more specialized content. Your voice teacher or vocal coach can continue your vocal instruction using them once you have learned and integrated the information presented here.

Training Your Voice

Most people would never participate in an athletic activity without taking some lessons to learn the basic skills to become successful. Singing is no different. The parts of the body primarily responsible for generating vocal sound are muscles capable of responding positively to physical training, and your voice will improve when they are strong, flexible, and working properly.

Developing Stamina and Strength

Unfortunately, many singers are frustrated with vocal problems and may fall victim to maladies such as injury, vocal strain, hoarseness, and even voice loss. A properly trained voice, on the other hand, can support the physical demands placed on it and avoid those problems. Would you play a sport without having trained your body to maintain a level of conditioning and endurance? Of course not! The same holds true with singing. You must properly prepare the parts of your body involved in vocal production so your voice is strong, healthy, and reliable.

The exercises themselves are muscle-movement based, and as long as you have a way to self-check, they are pretty straightforward and easy to learn and execute. In addition, this book focuses on developing new muscle memory primarily in the medium and low ranges, which creates a foundation upon which to build further vocal technique. In the same way as you train your muscles working out at a gym, you can train your singing muscles in the practice room.

Before You Start

This may sound a bit unusual, but some of you may need to seek a doctor's advice before beginning a vocal course of study, just as you might if you were beginning an exercise program at the gym. If you are having vocal problems you should determine the underlying cause. A trip to a knowledgeable, experienced laryngologist should be your first order of business. If possible, try to find a doctor who specializes in treating singers or public speakers.

During your appointment, be prepared for a full examination of your vocal cords. If there is physical problem, the doctor will be able to make that determination and explain it to you. The next step is to ascertain whether the problem(s) was due to illness, or caused by vocal abuse. That's a rather strong term for sure, but it's aptly descriptive, as vocal abuse is simply using your voice in such a way that it causes damage to the voice. The diagnosis might also indicate the need for some medical attention or speech therapy.

Always carefully consider the diagnoses and recommendations of medical experts. Laryngologists and speech therapists have training and experience, and they know the inner workings of the voice well. They can determine when, if, or how you should be using your voice. Please understand that *if you suffer from vocal problems, a laryngologist must clear you for singing* before you embark on any course of vocal training.

Once I had a student whose laryngologist told her she should take some voice lessons to improve her singing, in order to retrain her vocal habits to avoid incurring the same vocal problems. She immediately contacted me and arrived for her first lesson. Through the course of her lesson, I became more and more concerned, as her voice sounded very tough and she was having great difficulty reaching certain notes or producing any kind of a clear, free tone. It did not make sense to me, as she had said that the doctor had recommended the lessons.

A few days later, she went for a follow-up visit at her laryngologist's office, and they told her that she should not start voice lessons until she had finished her work with a speech therapist. Apparently, she had not understood from the initial appointment that the doctor had not *cleared her to sing*, but was suggesting the pursuit of proper vocal training subsequent to her recovery from the current state of vocal problems. Could you hurt your voice if you are singing when you should not? In short, the answer is yes. That is why it is so important to make sure that you are completely healthy when you begin your vocal training. If you are not careful, there is the potential to cause short-term or even permanent damage to your vocal cords by using them when they are not up to the job.

Baseline Assessment

Some speech therapists recommend that singers should consider having a baseline examination and imaging done of their vocal cords. Imaging your cords gives medical professionals a record they can compare to if you are sick or have vocal trouble in the future. Your doctor or speech therapist can help you determine if this is a good medical decision for your vocal health. These tests can be expensive, but if you are a professional singer, it might be something to consider. Some music schools regularly assess the vocal health of their incoming freshmen, in order to have this information available while they are in school.

The scope of vocal health is too broad for a discussion here, and so I prefer to leave that advice to those licensed, experienced physicians who specialize in the voice. When in doubt about a student's health, I always refer them to a professional laryngologist if there is any indication of vocal problems.

How to Use This Student Edition

This Student Edition is divided into two sections, a reference section containing information you will read either before, or after meeting with your voice teacher or vocal coach for a lesson. The information in each chapter will give you the knowledge you need to practice the exercises you learn in this course. You may find yourself re-reading the chapters in the first section of the book from time to time, to reinforce your knowledge and understanding of the concepts learned in your lessons.

The second section of this Student Edition contains your vocal exercises. They are in numerical order, and include short instructions to help you practice them correctly. Your voice teacher or vocal coach will teach the exercises in sequential order, and assign a corresponding Practice Plan to guide you in your practicing. This is the part of the book where you will spend most of your time.

The Vocal Fitness Studio Website: Things to Know

Accessing Resources at VocalFitnessStudio.com

With this book you will have 12 months of free online access to the 144 audio tracks, 30 instructional videos, and 40 Practice Plans through your smartphone, tablet or computer. In order to gain access, do the following:

1. **Visit: https://vocalfitnessstudio.com/pbonline**

2. Click or tap the "Add to Cart" button to add the Print Edition 1 Year Membership to your shopping cart.

3. **Enter the coupon code found on page 162 in the shopping cart to credit the full purchase price so you will get the 12-month membership for free.** You should see $0.00 on the Subtotal line.

4. Proceed to checkout. If you don't already have an account, you will set one up during checkout. You will have to provide your name and email address to set up your account and password to create access to this free content. Please note: it is not necessary to provide your phone number, even though the checkout page has that option displayed.

5. Complete the transaction and you will be given instructions on how to access the website resources with your account sign in. If you have any questions there is an email address on the receipt.

The Audio and Video Content and Practice Plans can be accessed through the Member Page at VocalFitnessStudio.com. Sign in to your account, and choose the link to access those pages.

Usernames and Passwords

Your username and password are managed by the shopping cart software (Cart66), and if you forget your username or password, there is Forget your password? help available at the sign in screen. Your username is the email address you used to set up your account to access the audio tracks, videos and Practice Plans. If you don't re-member your email, you can contact *Vocal Fitness Training* support through the contact tab at the website.

How to Practice the Spoken Exercises

Following are instructions that should be used for each exercise:

1. Take a moment to think about how you will incorporate all of the necessary movements and positions needed to create the best result, before speaking the exercise.

2. Speak the exercise while looking in a mirror. Repeat it a minimum of three times while focusing on the correct execution of the forms and positions taught in the lesson. Repeating the exercises in this way encourages the development of reflexive muscle memory. Think of this as the same as the reps you would do if you were lifting weights.

3. Continue the exercise provided you are sure that you have done the previous step accurately.

Remember that although vocal exercises come in many different patterns and flavors, the exercise is only effective if you practice it correctly. The exercises found in this book may seem simple, but they demand focus, concentration, and consistency in their execution to accomplish the best results.

How to Practice the Singing Exercises

The patterns for the singing exercise tracks are intentionally simple in order to give you the opportunity to practice efficiently with a prepared sequence. Most exercises present a chord played on a piano followed by a sung vocal model. Each exercise moves in a half-step fashion through the vocal range, but that does not mean that you sing the exercise example just once and then continue to the next example. When beginning any new exercise, follow these instructions:

1. Listen to the piano chord and the following sung example of the exercise pattern.

2. Once you hear the example, press Pause. (To help you to remember to pause,

3. there is a slight gap of silence between each vocal example.)

4. Take a moment to think about how you will incorporate all of the necessary movements and positions needed to create the best result, before singing the exercise.

5. Sing the exercise while looking in a mirror. Repeat the pattern on those pitches a minimum of three times while focusing on the correct execution of the forms and positions taught in the lesson. Repeating the exercises in this way encourages the development of reflexive muscle memory. Think of this as the same as the reps you would do if you were lifting weights.

6. When finished, press Play to continue the exercise, provided you are sure that you have done the previous step accurately.

Remember that although vocal exercises come in many different patterns and flavors, the exercise is only effective if you practice it correctly. The exercises found in this book may seem simple in their tunefulness, but they demand focus, concentration, and consistency in their execution to accomplish the best results.

Exercise Codes

All of the vocal exercises have letter codes assigned to them, which indicate the type of exercise.

A   Ascending most start on the A(4) above middle C and end on the D(5) an octave above middle C. Some of the later exercises will go higher, up to an F(5).

D   Descending most start on a G(4) above middle C and end up on the G(3) below it.

L   Low most start on a C major chord and end on a low E(3).

S   Spoken Exercises

V   Instructional Video

All exercises advance by ascending or descending half-steps and are sung in the female range (E3 to F5). In my experience, men should not have an issue with matching pitches in their ranges an octave below. One reason I did this was so that the chords and scale examples would be clear. Often times the lower range of the piano can sound muddy due to the lower frequencies, and make it harder to hear the pitches.

You may recall that the focus of this book is on developing the low, medium, and medium-high areas of the voice to create a strong vocal foundation. When you are singing these exercises, make sure you sing only as far as you are able to do so comfortably your range. You do not have to sing every chord pattern presented in the vocal exercise audio track when first starting out.

Introduction to Practice Plans

When I work with a personal trainer, I often ask for a list of exercises to do on my own. This helps to motivate me to stick to a regular routine. Periodically, I will change to a different workout to keep things interesting or to introduce new exercises.

It can be challenging to fit in all of our activities into our busy lives, and vocal practicing is no exception. Some years ago, I developed a series of vocal exercise routines similar in spirit to the ones that my personal trainer gave me, to help guide my students in their practicing. Giving them a predetermined practice plan frees them from having to figure out what to practice and allows them to use their time more efficiently.

The Practice Plans in this book focus primarily on the new concepts presented in your private lessons with your voice teacher or vocal coach. Each Practice Plan contains a sampling of previous exercises in order to work various aspects of your voice, including range building, vowel development, and vocal flexibility. Over time, you will develop a repertoire of vocal exercises that strengthen and maintain your vocal fitness.

Generally, the Practice Plans will contain four or more exercise tracks and present approximately a week's worth of practicing. The goal is to gain functional fitness, through daily exercise, so that the voice will respond easily to the challenges of the music you sing.

At first, the Practice Plans are set up to give you a minimum of four tracks to sing each day, generally resulting in fifteen to twenty-minute practice sessions, provided you sing a minimum of three times per example. Then, as you progress through the book, the number of tracks per day increases (and the length of your practice session along with that), but whether you will practice those additional tracks depends on your voice teacher or vocal coach. Remember, the goal is to practice a minimum of fifteen minutes per day to encourage the muscles to learn new positions and create muscle memory, and the Practice Plans help you to accomplish that by giving you a predetermined routine.

You will have access to these Practice Plans for one-year from the date you create your user account (for more information, see page 5). For your convenience, the Practice Plans can be accessed through the Member Page at VocalFitnessStudio.com. Sign in to your account, and scroll down to The Practice Room. Click on that link to go to the Practice Plans page.

Choose the Plan you wish to practice and click or tap the day of the week. It is recommended that you practice the exercises in the order presented in the playlist. These plans are mobile friendly and work on tablets and smartphones, and have the look and feel of an app.

If you would like to continue using the audio tracks after your membership expires, there are a few options available. They are available as monthly or yearly online subscriptions, or for purchase and download. The Practice Plans are not available, but instead, a similar Vocal Workout product offers either a monthly or yearly subscription. More information can be found at VocalFitnessStudio.com/store.

CHAPTER 1

WHAT IS VOCAL FITNESS?

This is the most important chapter you will read, because it outlines the basic concepts of what muscle fitness means for training your voice. Ultimately, nothing is new here in regards to presenting a progressive program of vocal exercises that improve your singing voice. What's different is the simple and straightforward approach to training your voice from a standpoint of muscle fitness, with the philosophy that proper physical vocal exercise unlocks the door to vocal improvement.

The Vocal Fitness Philosophy

Regardless of your level of experience, the overall design of Vocal Fitness Training will teach vocal technique efficiently. You will not find fancy or complicated exercises in this course. Rather, the scales and tunes of the exercises are simple so that you can focus on learning how to do them properly for the best outcome.

Remember, by deliberately focusing on progressive muscle training, Vocal Fitness Training goes beyond the traditional approach to teaching singing. When you look at it this way, it creates an entirely new paradigm of the process employed to improve your voice. By shifting the idea of vocal training to something tangible and attainable, it changes your understanding of what is possible. Confidence emerges as you gain an understanding of what steps you will take to improve your vocal production.

THE COMPONENTS OF SINGING

Since the ultimate goal is to improve the tone of your voice, you will need practice exercises that create the muscular strength to support the sustained tone of singing. First, though, here is a short overview of the basic components of vocal tone production.

Air

Air initiates the vocal sound, and the manner in which a singer both takes in and manages their breath is crucial to the success of the vocal sound. Although you already know how to coordinate air and phonation naturally for speech, singing demands more air pressure and breath management.

Vocal Cords

The vocal cords reside in your throat and, when air passes through them, they vibrate, initiating both sound and pitch. When exercised properly, the cords themselves and the surrounding muscle groups that control and support the larynx become stronger, more flexible, and responsive, balancing the vocal instrument.

Acoustic Resonance

The vocal tract is the area of your throat from the vocal cords to the lips. It's where acoustic resonance occurs, creating enhanced volume, tone, and vocal quality.

Articulation and Pronunciation

Often casually referred to as pronunciation, articulation is actually the movement and position of the tongue and lips which primarily affects the creation and/or modification of sounds within the mouth. The word *articulation* is the preferred description of internal mouth movement in this book, as it is a more precise descriptor of the muscle movements.

Pronunciation is a description of the way a word is spoken for clarity and understanding. An example of differing pronunciation occurs between British and American English. The words may have the same spelling, but they have different vowel and consonant sounds when pronounced. One of my favorite examples is the word *schedule*. In American English the "sch" sound is generally pronounced "sk," but in Britain it is often a "sh" sound. It may seem that pronunciation and articulation are interchangeable, but for the most part articulation will refer directly to muscle movement and pronunciation to how the word sounds.

THE ATHLETIC APPROACH

Vocal exercise is an athletic activity, since you are moving, stretching, conditioning, and strengthening muscles. The difference between singing and working out is that the muscles engaged for vocal production are much smaller than those larger groups you would train at the gym (e.g., quadriceps, biceps, or hamstrings). The focus is the same though, because we are also training for strength, stamina, endurance, and flexibility.

Well-trained muscles for singing easily produce clear tones throughout the range, improve the overall stamina of the voice, and bring the entire instrument into balance. However, like working out at the gym, you must regularly practice the exercises with the correct form and execution to realize these kinds of measurable results.

It is vitally important to understand that in order to strengthen and isolate specific muscles for singing, you must make sure that the form for the exercise is correct, including such things as lip posture, mouth shape, and tongue position. If your form and position is incorrect for any type of body exercise, there is risk for injury or for incomplete, ineffective, and inadequate muscle movement. The same thing holds true with vocal exercise. As long as the vocal instrument and its muscles are in proper alignment and balance during the exercise, there is less opportunity for either injury or poor vocal production.

Body-Weight and Resistance Training

Our goal is to stretch, strengthen, and engage the vocal-production muscle systems in a physical workout, but it does require a different approach than for other parts of the body. When we work out at the gym, we can challenge our muscles by using additional weights and resistance, such as dumbbells.

Certainly, we do not have any external weights we can use to train the muscles that operate our vocal instrument! However, there is an alternative—body-weight exercise. Using the body for strength training is a common approach widely used in traditional fitness workouts. Push-ups and squats are good examples of this, as they use the body's own weight to place force on the muscle to improve its strength. *Vocal Fitness Training*'s exercises use an approach similar to body-weight resistance training by challenging the right muscles and moving them through their full range of motion.

There are three distinct muscle groups that need our attention:

- Muscles used for the articulation of the vocal sound (tongue, lips, etc.)

- Muscles of the larynx and throat (including the vocal cords)

- Muscles used for respiration (rib, abdominal, diaphragm, etc.)

You can move some of these muscles intentionally, but you will have to learn to release others, so that their own unique movements will cause them to strengthen. These include, but are not limited to, the internal and external laryngeal and respiratory muscles. Vocal exercises, when done properly, will indirectly and reflexively move, stretch, and strengthen these muscles in coordination with vocalization.

With this approach, the muscles that you intentionally exercise create freedom for the others and encourage coordination of all three groups simultaneously. As you might imagine, it is very important to know where to focus your efforts in order to receive the best possible benefit, and *Vocal Fitness Training*'s exercises will guide you through this process.

DEVELOPING THE VOCAL FITNESS TRAINING™ METHOD

You will soon discover that one of the main strategies used in this curriculum to retrain a singer's muscle memory is the employment of exaggerated articulation and stretch. This may be an unfamiliar approach, and you may even be hesitant to use it; however, its intent is to jump-start your learning and create a path to better articulation and vocal tone. Following is the story of how I came to incorporate the application of exaggerated articulation as short-term strategy in my teaching method, and why it works.

A Sea-Change in My Voice Studio

Some years ago, I was teaching my students basic vocal exercises and assigning either standard classical repertoire or songs from the Golden Age of Broadway, depending on the student's interest. When shows like American Idol and The Voice became popular, I began to get inquiries for voice lessons from nonclassical singers who were singing pop, rock, R&B, gospel, and other genres.

Over the past 10 years, my studio has evolved to the point where my classical student population is smaller, and I now teach primarily musical theater and pop/rock artists; both amateurs and professionals who perform in many different venues. In fact, one of my students, Cara Watson, made it all the way through Hollywood Week on American Idol in 2014!

Retooling My Own Vocal Technique

During my classical and operatic training, I had one teacher who approached vocal development more pragmatically. The exercises we did were simple, with the intention of building the voice through deliberate changes in muscle movement and memory. This included a focus on articulation, because it directly influences many aspects of vocal tone production and allows for a firm anchoring of vocal utterance to the text.

At that time, my articulation and mouth positions were fine, but I needed improvement in the ability to sing with what my teacher described as "an active mouth." I had a habit of holding my mouth in a desired position to produce a proper singing tone. To improve, I learned to release those locked mouth positions with better muscle movement, and that activated my articulation.

Inactive Articulation

As I started working more with nonclassical singers, I noticed that many came into the studio with an almost complete lack of articulation. Without taking formal voice lessons, one can assume that an untrained singer may approach their singing with the articulation of regular speech. However, that kind of low energy articulation is inadequate if the singer wants to have more vocal strength and stamina.

Many popular music singers don't have a background in classical vocal training and sing however they deem is appropriate and satisfying for their style and genre. This can include vocal tones such as breathiness, grit, or nasality, which both the public and the recording industry deem acceptable forms of singing. Moreover, those vocal tones often lack good acoustic resonance, because those singers may be unaware of how to develop that to enhance their vocal sound. And since most sing with amplification, one could argue that there is little need to develop the voice beyond what is necessary to perform the song.

Many students came to me singing with inactive articulation and were unaware that it caused poor vocal habits like pushing, gripping, or singing from the throat which limited their singing abilities. Some were constantly losing their voices or were unable to gain more control and power over their voices. They reached out for help to find a way to solve these problems.

Creating a New Approach

The exercises I teach are effective and robust for training a classical voice and rely heavily on Italian vowel models from the traditional style of classical vocal training. As most of my nonclassical students sing primarily in American English, I decided to start with vocal exercises using three Italian vowel sounds: oh, oo, and ee, since they create a good foundation for active articulation and acoustic resonance. Even though we eventually do modify them to a more American English pronunciation, they provide an excellent place to begin improving their vocal tone and production.

Since the Italian vowel sounds created a purer and sometimes unfamiliar aural sound to the nonclassical students, I label the sound as the "Exercise Tone." The concept of the Exercise Tone is important to understand, because you will need to learn that practicing with these vowel positions will reap the most benefit.

However, the singing of completely pure Italian vowel sounds, or "Exercise Tone" is usually maintained only for the practicing of the vocal exercises. Later on, the active articulation gained from training on Italian vowel sounds results in an active mouth, allowing singers to create a beautiful vocal tone while preserving a more native version of colloquial American English. This helps to make each singer's sound uniquely their own.

Gently Stretching and Exaggerating the Italian Vowel Positions

The Italian vowel sounds successfully improved the students' mouth positions, but there still was a need to improve their overall articulation. To that end, I began to encourage them to stretch the articulation gently past the natural spoken position of the Italian vowel. The resulting stronger lip and facial positions positively affected the interior movements of the mouth (including the tongue), making it more active and encouraging better acoustic resonance, vocal tone, and volume.

These stronger movements redirected muscle movements away from the throat, which began to free it up and allowed those muscles to move more naturally. In addition, engaging the tongue while energetically articulating the vowels helped to eliminate the transfer of tension to the larynx. Overall, waking up and creating a more active mouth was making a measurable difference in vocal production.

What is Exaggerated Articulation?

First, we need to define *extreme* articulation: it is a muscle movement that stretches (or extends) the muscles to 100% of their ability. Unfortunately, that amount of movement is undesirable for singing since it risks hyperextension and overexertion of the muscles and joints.

Instead, you will need to extend and stretch the muscle movements as far as you can without locking or creating excess tension. It should not be painful, and if a you feel that you are overdoing the movement, you should stop immediately and rest the muscles. Nothing is gained by forcing the muscle movement.

You should try to stretch your muscles gently to a position that is no further than 80-85% of the undesirable extreme articulation movement. Any movement that strives to reach that range of 80-85% of stretching we define as *exaggerated articulation*. You should challenge your muscles, but never strain, tire, or overdo the movement, but instead ask your body for a gentle, insistent stretch. At first, you may only be able to stretch a little past normal speech positions, but with practice, the flexibility will increase.

Using the idea of a percentage of stretch (80-85%) as a guideline is not measurable, but it intends to communicate the goal of working the muscles to an approximate position to achieve the desired result of strength and flexibility. Using exaggerated articulation and stretching the Italian vowel positions to activate the mouth and create better acoustic resonance means that singers rarely need to know how to manipulate their mouth shapes to the desired vowel positions, but can base their articulation on a more natural model.

Exercise through Exaggeration

Most people do not realize what a large part pronunciation and articulation play in actual vocal production. Strong, exaggerated positions for speech aid greatly in creating a solid foundation for singing. Without this type of active and strong articulation from the mouth, the entire instrument will collapse, resulting in substandard and potentially unhealthy vocal production.

Since the singing voice is a natural extension of speech, the most direct way to improve our singing voice is to enhance and exaggerate speech to the point where it becomes sustained, pitched tones. Try this: speak the following sentence in extremely slow motion by exaggerating the consonants and dragging out the length of the vowel sounds.

O___ say___ ca___n you___ see___

By___ the___ daw___n'sear___ly___ li___ght

Wha___tso___prou___dly___we___hai___led

A___t the___ twi___li__ght's

la___st glea__mi___ng

Notice how the slow, exaggerated pronunciation creates a sound similar to monotone singing. If we add pitch, duration, and rhythm to this text, it will become a very recognizable song.

To create resistance against our articulator muscles, you will need to engage movement that is a natural part of the singing (and speaking) process. When we exaggerate the proper pronunciation of vowels and consonants, it stretches and challenges our muscles as they resist an unfamiliar, extreme movement.

This is where we can see a similarity to body-weight resistance training in traditional workouts, as these exaggerated positions gently stretch the muscles past the normal range of motion used for speech. This conditions the muscles as they gain strength, tone, balance, and fitness, eventually giving the singer the ability to sustain a beautiful tone with a minimum of physical effort.

Muscles and Acoustic Resonance

The casual observer might think that voice training focuses on the development of the vocal cords, and it does to some extent. However, good tone production is due in large part to the quality of the sound waves that develop in the throat and mouth after the initial sound comes from the vocal cords. Many of the muscles we target for vocal exercise are the ones primarily responsible for creating the positions that assist with acoustic-resonance development. The strength and flexibility of these muscles leads to long-term endurance, which in turn creates a consistent and healthy vocal tone.

Developing Muscle Endurance

People who go to the gym generally work out with exercises that fall into three main categories: strength (weight lifting), cardiovascular (aerobics), and flexibility (yoga). A related area of strength training, muscle endurance, is different from conventional strength workouts, as the goal is to develop the ability of a muscle to sustain repetitive stress over a long period without fatiguing. Muscle-endurance exercises increase repetitions using lighter weights, and they do not have a goal of pushing the muscle until it fails, but rather they focus on developing stamina.

Vocal Fitness Training's exercises use the concepts of muscle endurance and strength training *without pushing muscles to fatigue.* As singing muscles become able to maintain their shape and form while singing, your ability to generate a consistent and smooth singing tone is enhanced. Singers, therefore, should be very interested in developing endurance, as it helps to improve vocal stamina, but they should never push their muscles to fail.

Muscle Strengthening with Vowels

Since muscle movement and position determine the best vocal output, we need to utilize what is available to us to work out the muscles. The concept of using sustained vowel sounds as the cornerstone of developing the voice has been around for centuries. Practically all vocal exercises are sung on vowels because they are your primary vocal tone.

Is Singing Relaxing?

When you reach a point in your voice study where everything starts to work properly, it may begin to feel relaxing. This is generally due to the absence of muscle tension gained from better vocal technique. You may feel as if you are relaxed while singing compared to your old habits. You might even feel as if you have an open throat, because now there is a lack of tension in the neck. However, the absence of tension and gripping in this case is not a relaxed vocal production, but a balanced one. When you learn how to engage the muscles properly, there is no relaxation because you will never release your articulation. Each syllable you sing will have energy and life until you finish the phrase or pause to breathe. Think of riding a bicycle recreationally where you pedal and coast, pedal and coast. In singing, there is no coasting; *you are always pedaling!*

STRONG, EXAGGERATED PRONUNCIATION: A MEANS TO AN END

With practice, you can enhance and increase the energy expended with the muscles in the mouth by using progressive exercises that initially exaggerate pronunciation. This approach retrains and creates new habits of muscle movement by stretching and engaging muscles to produce an easily sung and solid vocal tone.

Before you embark on this course of study, it is important to understand completely that strong, exaggerated articulation is a *means to an end*. The exercises are just that, exercises. *Vocal Fitness Training*'s exercises use strong, exaggerated articulation as an opening strategy to create the best results. As you gain strength and flexibility, the muscles will begin to hold their positions easily, the strong, exaggerated articulation will decrease, and the external production of vowels and consonants will look and sound natural.

At the outset, it may seem that *Vocal Fitness Training*'s exercises look a little silly when viewed in a mirror. Remember, the short-term goal is to use this type of exaggeration to encourage the development of a stronger, flexible, and more responsive instrument. You need to use whatever you have available to challenge the muscles, which is the resistance offered by strong, exaggerated articulation.

This approach is similar to the concept of functional fitness, where physical training focuses on the results that positively influence everyday tasks. For instance, someone who is able to lift a twenty-five-pound weight at the gym will have no difficulty at the grocery store lifting a gallon of milk weighing eight pounds, as their arm has been strengthened by lifting a heavier weight. Setting a goal of functional fitness for singing is similar, because as your muscles become stronger from the use of the exaggerated stretch, your singing will become easier.

CHAPTER 2

Introduction to Strong, Exaggerated Articulation

Many classical singers learn to sing with vowels as a way to train and strengthen their voices. Borrowing from those established vocal-training traditions, you will learn three primary vowels for your initial exercises, /oo/, /oh/, and /ee/, which build a foundation for a stronger vocal sound.

Practical Vocal Science

Vocal Fitness Training focuses on strengthening the muscles that articulate the vowels. Many students who come to my studio often underutilize the movements of the mouth and face in vocal production, causing improper vowel positioning. To solve that problem, you need to learn how to release the articulating muscles of the mouth through repositioning. This will entail creating vowel sounds from the natural pronunciation positions of speech.

Creating vocal tones involves many reflexive muscle movements hidden from our sight. When our thoughts indicate that we want to sing a certain note and word, muscles respond to that request automatically and produce the vowels and consonants required. We are able to override some of these instructions consciously, but, if done incorrectly, we run the risk of creating unwanted tension in the voice.

Practical exercise Preparation

Muscle Positioning for Vowels

There are charts and diagrams that map the position of the tongue for each vowel sound that are sometimes helpful to voice teachers and singers to gain a deeper understanding of the underlying process of tongue positioning. However, I rarely use them with students, since everyone already knows how to pronounce their vowels. Instead, I focus on developing a stronger vowel and adjusting for regional accents, when necessary and appropriate.

Vocal Fitness Training's exercises rely on standard vowel pronunciations because they directly influence your tone quality. Once you begin to produce good tone quality, you can integrate your musical style with it. For example, if you sing country music, which favors a twangy sound, you will simply alter the pronunciation of the vowels to favor the country accent inherent in the style of this music. This would include such things as nasality, twang, or drawl. The goal is to give you a basic tone that you can bend and shape to your vocal style, but, most importantly, you will retain your signature sound, so that you only sound like you. In my studio, I strive to maintain the style of the singer, as there is no one-size-fits-all sound. As you practice these exercises in your voice, your body will define the results as they relate to your own personal characteristics.

Ideally, you would address the integration of your vocal style after you have finished working through the exercises in this book. Generally, a commitment to working solely on technique is well worth it because it establishes new muscle memory that will ultimately replace your old vocal habits.

Vowel Symbols

Throughout this book, you will see vowels represented by symbols surrounded by forward slashes (/). These symbols convey the pronunciation of the vowel sound in standard American English.

Any phonetic symbol is useful if it conveys meaning to the reader, and there are many ways to symbolize vowel sounds, but my intention is to keep things as simple as possible. For that reason, most of the symbols used in this book are intuitive, such as /ee/ for the vowel sound in the word *fleece*. For those readers who are interested in learning a more complete and formal symbol set, I encourage them to study the International Phonetic Alphabet (IPA). The IPA is the standard pronunciation key for many foreign languages of the world.

Comparing Mouth Positions of Vowels

The following activities demonstrate how the unique positions of the mouth, lips, and tongue influence the quality of the vowel sounds.

Forward Stretch

Say /oo/ (as in the word *goose*) each time with a different mouth position. Each of these positions produces an /oo/ sound, but you will find that the third example produces the best overall vocal tone.

- Smile broadly and say /oo/.

- Relax the smile and the tongue and say /oo/.

- Purse your lips as if you were going to whistle and say /oo/.

Horizontal Stretch

Try the same experiment for the vowel sound /ee/ (as in the word *fleece*). Notice that the last position with a broad smile produces the best tone.

- Purse your lips as if you were going to whistle and say /ee/.

- Relax your mouth and the tongue and say /ee/.

- Smile broadly and say /ee/.

As you have seen, when you purse your lips in an exaggerated forward position, the strongest and purest tone occurs for the /oo/ vowel. It is similar to the position for whistling or the strong muscle stretch for sipping a very thick milkshake through a straw. The tongue automatically engages in a strong, stretched position, with the inner surfaces of the lips tucked in.

You may notice a slight hollowing of the cheeks caused by the stretching of your facial muscles. The key is to feel this stretch inside your mouth and to observe the resulting space that opens up naturally. You must learn this strong articulation position of the /oo/ properly, because it teaches you the combination of both a strong stretch and the proper positioning of the muscles.

Launching Vowel Exercises with the Consonant Sound "y"

Many of the vocal exercises begin with a strong initiation of the "y" consonant sound as in the English word *ye*. A strong voicing of this consonant helps to engage and strengthen the tongue. It also encourages a continued stretch as it helps to transfer energy from the tongue to the lips as they move into a strong forward position.

The strong articulation that occurs when you pronounce the "y" consonant causes the sides of the back of your tongue to press strongly against the inside of your upper molars. Its strong articulation helps to push off the vowel, in much the same way a competitive swimmer pushes off from the side of the pool after a turn. To emphasize this, linger for a moment as you begin to produce the "y" sound and then glide into the /oo/.

You may hear a small /ee/ sound produced when pronouncing the "y." This naturally occurs as the consonant engages the tongue in the approximate position of the /ee/ vowel. This is fine, at first, but as you gain more ability with this consonant-vowel combination the goal will be to glide quickly to the /oo/. You will see a similar situation with any pairing using "y" and a vowel.

CHAPTER 3

How the Voice Works: A Vocal Production Primer

This chapter introduces the basic functioning of the vocal apparatus as it relates to singing. This chapter does not present any vocal exercises. Physiological, acoustic, and scientific principles that govern vocal production are the foundation of *Vocal Fitness Training*. In this chapter, you will learn how your body produces a singing tone in order to gain a broad understanding and practical knowledge of how the vocal apparatus works.

Practice Vocal Science

Reflexive Muscle Memory

Vocal production relies on a series of complex muscle movements and positions, and yet it all seems to happen automatically when we speak. Without any conscious muscular effort, our strong desire to communicate moves the muscles into the correct positions to pronounce a word as a direct response to our thoughts.

When training the voice, we strive to have the muscles work as naturally as they do in speech, initiating their movements through what I call reflexive muscle memory. To understand this concept, let us take a close look at the sequence of muscle movements in our mouths when we speak a single word. For this example, we will examine the production of the syllables in the word *important*.

	Air vibrates the vocal cords, initiating vocal sound, which travels up into the throat and mouth.
im	The throat and tongue move to produce the vowel sound /ih/, and the lips close to the /m/, completing the first syllable.
por	Air builds up behind the lips, and the consonant /p/ explodes with a puff of air, and the throat and tongue quickly move into position to produce the /ohr/ vowel sound for the second syllable /por/.
ta	The tongue touches and springs back from the roof of the mouth, creating a puff of air for the consonant /t/, and the throat and tongue move to produce the vowel sound /ă/ of the third syllable.
nt	The tongue moves to the roof of the mouth behind the front teeth and produces the consonant /n/ as the tongue stays on the roof of the mouth and releases, creating a puff of air for the consonant /t/ finishing the word.

Whew, all of those muscle movements for just one word! Thankfully, these complicated movements for each vowel and consonant happen below the level of consciousness, relying on the muscle memory that you retained when learning to speak. Every word you utter has an imbedded memory of the sequence of movements needed to create it, and they occur as a response to your thoughts as reflexive muscle memory.

Since singing is essentially an extension of speech, enhancing this type of reflexive movement is helpful in producing consistent and strong vocal tones. First, you need to explore the components that produce vocal sound. Some of you may already be familiar with the way the voice works, however, I encourage you to read this section as it will act as a refresher and will introduce you to terminology used in this book.

The Vocal Cords

Vocal folds is the most correct and accurate scientific term for the muscle pair in our throat that initiates vocal sound. However, since most people know them by their more common label, *vocal cords*, we will refer to them as such in this book.

The vocal cords are made of several layers of muscle tissue, which gives them both flexibility and strength. They reside just above the trachea within a flexible structure called the *larynx* (commonly known as the voice box). The following graphic shows the basic structure of the throat and mouth, including the location of the larynx where the vocal cords reside.

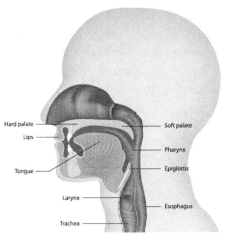

In addition to producing vocal tone, the vocal cords also function as a valve that opens for breathing (respiration) and closes to prevent food from entering the lungs (protection). Viewed from above, they appear as two distinct muscle sections with a thin edge. When open, this resembles a slight upside-down *V* shape stretched from the front to the back of the larynx.

VOCAL CORD

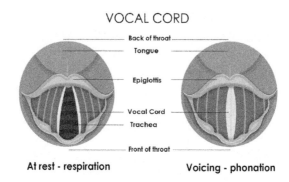

At rest - respiration   **Voicing - phonation**

At rest (respiration), the vocal cords remain apart, and when they are ready to generate sound, they will come together and close. When enough air pressure builds up underneath the closed vocal cords, they burst apart with a puff of sound and immediately return to their closed position. This cycle of opening and closing occurs many times per second as the air continues to flow between them, creating a vibrating *fundamental pitch*.

Players of brass instruments can create a similar fundamental sound by buzzing their lips on a mouthpiece. The fundamental pitch produced by the vocal cords, however, is a direct result of their length. Although a brass player can make some minor alterations of pitch with their lips, vocal cords have the unique ability to create a myriad of different pitches since they can change their length significantly.

Approximate vocal cord positions for high and low notes

Shortened cord = low note   Extended cord = high note

As the vocal cords lengthen and thin, they vibrate faster, creating a high pitch. Conversely, when they shorten and thicken, the vibrations are slow, producing a *low* pitch. Even though there are other muscular movements involved in the process that assist the vocal cords, this is enough information for now to give you a basic understanding of their movement and role in producing sound.

This is another example of reflexive muscle memory. When the vocal cords create the initial fundamental pitch, the larynx stretches the cords by moving to the correct position and proper length for the desired pitch as a reflexive response. The vocal cords then vibrate as the air flows over them. Fortunately, you do not have to control these muscle movements consciously other than desiring to sing a certain pitch.

THE LARYNX

The vocal cords reside in the larynx, which is composed of interlocking cartilages and bone connected by membranes, ligaments, and muscles. The most recognizable and largest of the cartilages is the thyroid, which is somewhat prominent in men, in whom it is commonly known as the Adam's apple. The larynx is flexible and capable of rapid movement and changes in position.

LARYNX

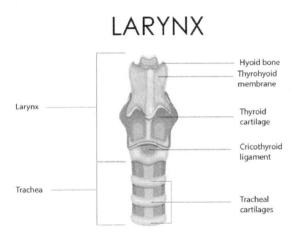

Both internal and external muscles control its movements and assist with positioning the larynx and the vocal cords properly to produce pitch. Since most of the larynx's movement is reflexive, interference with these muscles can unbalance it, creating a great deal of tension within the vocal mechanism. Learning good vocal technique will help you achieve the correct balance and contribute to healthy vocal production.

Internal Laryngeal Muscles

There are many complex interior laryngeal muscle movements, which are primarily responsible for moving the vocal cords together and generating suitable tension for vocal sound production. Further discussion of these complex internal movements is not critical because your thoughts primarily guide their reflexive movements.

External Laryngeal Muscles

There are many neck and throat muscles involved in vocal production, some of which manage the movement of the larynx. Although you do not want to manipulate these muscles directly, you do need to develop the skills to give them the freedom to operate and function naturally in conjunction with the rest of the vocal instrument.

The important thing for you to remember is that the larynx is in constant motion as it moves to appropriate positions for producing singing or speech sounds. Not all of the external laryngeal muscles are involved directly in the production of sound. However, if they are impeded it can influence the movement of the interior muscles, inhibiting the movement of the vocal cords. Unbalanced posture, head position, neck and jaw tension, breath, and relaxed or tense articulation are examples of the types of behaviors that may impinge on the natural movements of the larynx.

An example of incorrect muscle movement occurs if a singer juts their head up and forward when singing a high note or leans forward, tucking in their chin, for a very low note. These particular movements can have a detrimental effect on both head position and neck posture as they stress the external muscles around the larynx and transfer that negative energy to the vocal apparatus. Fortunately, these are all things that you can correct or manage, keeping the external laryngeal muscles free to function properly.

THE TONGUE

The tongue is a very large muscle connected to many other muscles groups in the jaw and throat, including the hyoid bone, from which the larynx is suspended. Because of the interconnectivity of the tongue and the larynx, improper movement of the tongue has the potential to influence many aspects of vocal production negatively. For example, if the tongue is too relaxed or too tense when singing, it can hinder the mobility of the larynx.

The tongue greatly influences vocal production because of how its position and height play a vital role in the creation of vowel sounds. Most people are familiar with the tongue's obvious role in pronouncing consonants near the front of the mouth (i.e., *t, p*, etc.). However, vowel positioning engages the sides, middle, and even the base of the tongue (near the back of the throat).

During your vocal study, focusing on tongue positions does not necessarily need a lot of specific attention because you already know how to speak, and you learned the basic vowel formations when you acquired speech. Our primary concern with the tongue is to make sure that you engage it through strong articulation, so that it remains active. You need to avoid both a relaxed or tense tongue, conditions which can create vocal tension and/or reduce the amount of resonance in the tone.

The Relaxed Tongue

One of two misconceptions often leads to issues with a relaxed tongue: The first is that singing is a relaxed activity, and the other is that the energy levels one uses for speech are adequate for vocal production. If a person sings without engaging enough energy in the mouth, that habit will influence vocal production negatively by weighing down the rest of the instrument. A relaxed tongue means that the singer has articulation that causes the back of the tongue to sink into the pharynx on the inside or press against the throat muscles on the outside, thereby inhibiting or interfering with their movements.

The Tense Tongue

The problem of a tense tongue affects laryngeal function by pulling the tongue up and away from its natural position. There are a number of causes, including improper mouth positions in the higher range of the voice, holding the tongue while singing a long sustained tone, and moving or positioning the tongue to manipulate vowel positions. Lack of proper breath management including singing to the end of the breath can also cause the tongue to tense, as the singer attempts to produce vocal sound at any cost.

Exercising the Tongue Muscles

All of the exercises in this course of study use vowel and consonant articulation so there is an intentional focus on exercising the tongue and its muscles. Some vocal methods will work to release the tongue through isolated muscular exercises, but the goal here is to coordinate and integrate vocal production using the voice as part of the exercise. The tongue needs to be flexible and have the ability to stretch and move. Properly executed vocal exercises using both vocal sounds and exaggerated stretch will help to accomplish those goals.

Soft Palate

The soft palate (or velum) is located at the back of the roof of the mouth. When it rises, it closes off the opening to the nasal passages during swallowing. It also raises and lowers during the pronunciation of vowels. When raised, more sound flows into the mouth, preventing the nasality caused by sound waves traveling unrestricted into the nasal passages.

The lifting of the palate in singing is a common strategy to improve baseline vocal tone. The keys are to strengthen the muscles that help lift it up naturally through vocal exercises and to develop a natural stretch that becomes a part of the muscle memory of singing.

VOCAL TRACT: THE PRIMARY ACOUSTIC RESONATOR

The term *vocal tract* refers to the area from the vocal cords to the lips, and its path includes the interior of the pharynx and the mouth (indicated by the white line in the drawing below). This part of the vocal instrument has acoustic-resonance properties that modify or change the fundamental pitch into vocal tone.

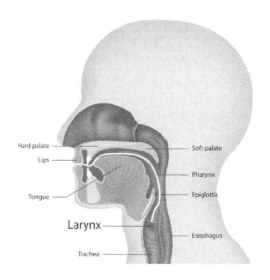

To understand this process, it is necessary to take a very brief overview of the physics of vocal sound. A scientific discussion about this subject can be extremely complex; however, it is a good idea to understand the basic functions of acoustics as they apply to the vocal tract, since they are instrumental in the production of singing tone. The following description is intended to be a brief and simple introduction of acoustics as they occur in the vocal tract, and it is by no means intended to be a scientifically complete description of what is truly a very complicated subject to discuss. Why is this so helpful to know? If you understand that the shape of your vocal tract influences singing tone quality, then you can focus on learning how to do this properly in a consistent manner.

Please remember that there is a point where vocal science merely explains the process and results of vocal production and the application of scientific knowledge does not always directly enhance your vocal training. On the other hand, a reasonable amount of knowledge about the inner workings of your voice helps you to understand the reason for focusing on particular aspects of vocal technique better.

Frequencies and Harmonics

Frequency describes the rate that an object vibrates in cycles per second, or Hz, (a term honoring the famous physicist Heinrich Hertz). We generally describe these vibrations as pitch, but they also have an assigned frequency number. For example, if you sing a G above middle C, it means that your vocal cords are vibrating at approximately 400 Hz (or 400 times per second!).

Once that fundamental frequency or pitch of 400 Hz emanates from your vocal cords, it produces a type of sound wave (periodic) that sets into motion a series of additional simultaneous frequencies called *harmonics* or *harmonic overtones*. Harmonic frequencies created from a fundamental pitch follow a predictable mathematical sequence as integer multiples (1, 2, 3, etc.). This is easy to explain, as it is simply a matter of multiplication. For example, if the fundamental frequency produced by the vocal cords is 400 Hz, then we know the frequency of the basic harmonic overtones:

- The first harmonic overtone will be 800 Hz (the fundamental pitch of 400 Hz x 2 = 800).

- The second will be 1200 Hz (400 x 3 = 1200).

- The third at 1600 Hz, and so on.

All of these additional simultaneous frequencies are present in the sound as it leaves the vocal cords and travels through the vocal tract, making the tone sound richer. Without these harmonics, our musical tones would be pretty dull and uninteresting.

Resonance

Scientifically, the discussion of resonance can be quite complicated and involves mathematical formulas and physics to study the properties of sound waves and their behavior within a resonating structure. For now, we just need to know that the way the sound reverberates inside the vocal tract enhances or improves the vocal tone in quality and volume. Since the acoustic resonator of the voice is our vocal tract, altering its position and shape changes the sound of your singing either positively or negatively.

Fortunately, we can assume some control over those aspects of vocal production and positively influence and enhance the resonance qualities within the vocal tract.

Filtering

Filtering is a result of the function of resonance properties that occur in the acoustic space of the vocal tract. Since areas of the vocal tract have the capability to change shape, the vocal tract filters the sound frequencies traveling through it. Filtering can cause the removal or dampening of some of the harmonics (the additional frequencies described above), which help in the creation of specific vocal tones. For example, as the vocal tract changes shape, it modifies the vocal output for producing vowel sounds as well as altering the tone and timbre of the vocal output.

VOCAL REGISTERS

There are several terms and concepts which describe vocal mechanics and production.

- *Register*: Simply put, a *register* is a collection of successive pitches.

- *Laryngeal Positioning*: Scientific observation has determined that there are predictable places in the vocal cords and larynx where specific physical positions occur as they produce pitch. These include the amount of the vocal cord involved in the vibration and the physical movement of the larynx itself.

- *Vocal Register*: This term describes the range of successive notes contained within any of the laryngeal positions.

- *Register Change*: This is the spot in the vocal range where laryngeal changes occur. People often incorrectly label them as *breaks* in the voice, even though nothing is actually broken. Instead, these refer to the body's own repositioning of the larynx and vocal cords for the next set of pitches. Generally, if you hear a flip or skip in a singer's voice at the register change, it means that they have not had the proper training and they have not developed their voice well enough to sing through their register changes smoothly. Further, they might try to maintain the incorrect laryngeal position for the notes that they are attempting to sing.

- *Names of the Registers*: Both vocal scientists and pedagogues have a variety of names for the registers. The most common terminology organizes the voice into two defined groups: *head voice* and *chest voice*. Other register descriptions may include *vocal fry, falsetto, mode 1, mode 2,* and *whistle,* to name a few.

Regardless of what name you give a vocal register, it is more important to understand what they are and how that knowledge can help you further your vocal study. Following is a very short discussion of the four most common register descriptions you will encounter.

HEAD AND CHEST VOICE?

Of all the terms that describe vocal production, head and chest voice are probably the most grossly inaccurate in describing the actual physiological workings of the larynx and vocal cords. Since vocal tone originates from the vocal cords, it is impossible to place or direct its origination from any other part of your body, such as your head or chest. However, those parts of our body do vibrate when making vocal tones; the lower tones are felt in the chest and the higher pitches in the head. This type of perceived vibration is likely why these terms originated and persist today.

There is further confusion because these are also terms for describing the first and second registers of the voice. To make matters more confusing, others label these registers with such terms as *mode 1* and *mode 2, low voice* and *high voice, heavy* and *light mechanism, speech* and *loft voice, thin* and *thick,* and so on. In the end, it really does not matter what you call them, but it is important to understand that the register name describes a range of successive notes in your voice produced by a particular physical positioning and the thickness of the cords. In addition, misconceptions about how to access these registers abound, because of these ambiguous labels.

Chest Voice

The term *chest voice* is probably the one that causes the most problems. A fair amount of the chest register contains the notes of our speaking voice and utilizes most of the vocal cord, creating a rich set of harmonics. The problem occurs when a singer tries to maintain that dark, rich sound and physically manipulates their voice by pushing through the register shift to try to carry the heavier tone throughout their range. That is difficult to do because it works against the natural inclination of the larynx to switch gears and change position for higher notes. This can result in a bigger and more obvious break in the voice when it finally gives up under the pressure of maintaining the wrong physical position. This is similar to keeping a car in low gear and refusing to shift to a higher gear, putting stress on the engine. Overworking the vocal cords this way can also cause long-term vocal strain and fatigue in the muscles, which has the potential to lead to vocal problems.

Head Voice

Another misperception is that head voice is a lighter, or even a breathy, tone. The term *head voice* generally refers to a higher pitch set that occurs at the second register change, which means that the intention of the term is not to describe vocal *quality*. Its lighter sound is sometimes rightly indicative of the higher frequencies and harmonics produced (and certainly not from it emanating from any part of the head). Even though an untrained voice can exhibit light and breathy properties, it is inaccurate to use the term *head voice* as a descriptor of vocal qualities.

In some circles, you may also hear the head voice called *falsetto*, which is a term only appropriate to a register change and physical repositioning that occurs in men's voices. The use of the term *falsetto* for women's voices is functionally incorrect, since there is no physical movement or change of position occurring in women's larynxes as it does in men's voices. A poorly produced female head voice may share similar qualities to the male falsetto, as it may exhibit a thinner, lighter sound than their normal voice.

Mixed Voice

Then there is the popular term, *mixed voice*, which seems to indicate that you can combine the two registers together. In reality, you cannot combine the registers because by definition they describe separate and distinct physical laryngeal movements. A well-trained voice can produce balanced resonance, though, resulting in vocal output that sounds like a mix of the dark, heavy chest voice and the lighter sounding head voice. The fact is that good vocal training will create a balanced tone or "mixed" voice, so there is really no need to distinguish that as a special vocal production, technique, or register.

Falsetto

Falsetto is a register designation unique to the male voice where the length and thickness of the vocal cords changes, producing a tone that allows them to sing at least an octave higher than their normal full voice.

Most men find their falsetto easily, by playing around with higher notes, and interestingly there is generally an overlap where men can sing pitches using either their full voice or their falsetto. Most musical styles will draw on falsetto to access very high pitches, especially since many baritones or basses may not be able to sing those notes in their regular singing voice. If men sing in a style requiring the use of their falsetto voice, then they can practice using the same vocal exercises as they do for their full voice, including the breath-management techniques.

Defining Registers in this Book

There is a generally accepted range of notes where register changes occur in both male and female voices, but it can vary slightly from singer to singer. Our task is to observe where these changes occur in our own voices and realize that register changes are a natural occurrence that can be improved and managed with vocal training.

VOCAL ONSET AND STYLISTIC CHOICES

Vocal onset describes how the vocal sound begins, and ideally it results from breath pressure building up underneath the vocal cords blowing them apart naturally, causing them to vibrate and create sound.

However, if the air pressure beneath the vocal cords is either too little or too great, other muscles may engage to help, consequently causing unwanted tension in the larynx or tongue, constricting the vocal cords, and ultimately impeding their ability to vibrate freely. Instead of opening and closing evenly, the edges of the vocal cords may become irritated as they hit or rub against each other, and they may even swell. This may lead to incomplete closure, or a host of other problems, like gripping and tightening of the surrounding muscles or causing pain in the throat. In the end, this kind of pervasive muscular movement is unhealthy and has the potential to lead to vocal problems.

Some singers who seem to have extremely durable vocal cords rarely seem to suffer any consequences from improper vocal onset, but they are the exception and not the rule. Keep in mind that every set of vocal cords is different and some are simply stronger and thicker than others and can take more abuse. Singers who use amplification can also get away with some improper vocal onset as they rely heavily upon the microphone and sound system to project their voices.

However, if a singer uses faulty vocal onset for extended periods, it can become problematic for them, regardless of the use of amplification. Used sparingly in some styles of singing, a few of the onsets described below are not necessarily harmful or damaging to the voice, and in certain styles of music are accepted as legitimate vocal sounds. On the other hand, excessive and long-term use of these onsets has the potential to place strain on the vocal cords, which may put them at risk for vocal injury. I strongly advise only intentional, infrequent, and judicious use of these vocalizations for stylistic purposes. All *Vocal Fitness Training's* exercises avoid these onsets because they are not part of a healthy vocal training regimen.

Glottal Stop

Glottal Stop is a sound caused by the vocal cords coming together to stop the flow of air. The consonant sound "k" is a good example of this. Another commonly used glottal stop is found in the phrase "uh-oh," where the first syllable of "uh" is stopped before it is continued by the voiced "oh" sound. Since the cords are closed, starting a tone from a glottal stop creates friction that can irritate the vocal cords and causes an unnecessary amount of air pressure to build up underneath them.

Vocal Fry

Vocal Fry is a common onset heard in popular and rock music, and it sounds like a creaking door. Voice scientists categorize vocal fry as the lowest register of the voice, where its physical mechanism simultaneously compresses and relaxes the vocal cords creating an irregular popping sound. This vocalization makes it more difficult to glide into the normal singing tone and disrupts the natural movement of the vocal cords.

Growl

Growl occurs mostly in heavier styles of popular and rock music. It is irritating to the vocal cords as it is often produced in the same manner as clearing your throat (which essentially rubs and slams your vocal cords together). The heaviest styles of music like heavy metal go a step further and take it to the unhealthy level of screaming.

Rasp or Grit

You will hear singers with raspy or gritty voices in many forms of popular music. There are a myriad of reasons for this, ranging from vocal abuse to medical issues like vocal cord nodules or even illness. The reason these singers are able to produce this quality may only come to light from a medical examination of their vocal cords by a laryngologist. Unfortunately, raspy singing can be very unhealthy, and prolonged use of this style carries the potential to cause permanent damage. There have been recording artists who have used this voice quality to great success, however, we will probably never know if they had vocal problems along the way. Some rock singers have damaged vocal cords, and that may be what ultimately gives them their signature sound!

Currently, the music industry seems to like and encourage some of these sounds, and it promotes singers who use it. The acceptance of these rough vocal sounds by the listener may stem from a perception that they convey high levels of emotion within the vocal performance. That may be the case, but, over time, it has become a style of singing, and singers who make these sounds often give the impression that they are screaming their music. Physically our voices are not built to take that type of constant vocal abuse, and it is an interesting question as to why these gravelly, rough sounds, which normally would fall into the spectrum of screaming, have become so popular. I had a student once who sang in a heavy metal band, and he regularly screamed (not in my studio, although he did share some recordings with me), but it did not seem to have any negative effect on his singing voice when he was at his lessons. On the other hand, I taught some rock singers who have needed help retooling their singing to keep them from getting sore throats or losing their voices after performances.

Caution is key here. Even my heavy metal rocker student knew the value in training his legit voice to give him some solid vocal technique.

If you do decide that you need to explore raspy singing, you do so at your own risk—as with any of the vocal onsets that fall outside of the healthy realm of vocal production. Nevertheless, remember, if it hurts when you use any of the above vocalizations, you are probably irritating the vocal cords, and you could place yourself at risk of doing short or long-term damage.

CONTEMPORARY COMMERCIAL MUSIC

For many years, vocal instruction focused on formal training of the voice for classical music. Vocal music that did not fall into that category was generally labeled *non-classical*, and included such genres as musical theater, pop, rock, folk, country, jazz, and blues. Recently, many singers are adopting the term Contemporary Commercial Music (CCM) for these styles of singing as a group. There has been recent acknowledgment that these singing styles deserve attention from voice teachers, and many have begun to teach, research, and develop vocal techniques to address them.

Much of the style of CCM is speech based, with the theatricality of the music demanding a naturally produced vocal sound. Vocal style is a subject too broad for this book, but if you are a CCM singer, you are already aware of the kinds of vocalizations expected, such as twang in country music. Muscle conditioning and vocal fitness are the focuses of this book, without a bias toward any one genre of singing; it is intended to give you a strong vocal foundation upon which you can build your vocal style.

For those who sing musical theater, it is necessary to have a strong vocal foundation to be able to switch between the varied styles of singing required. If you are fortunate enough to get a job on the Broadway stage, you will need to have the vocal stamina, technique, and strength to sustain performing effectively in eight shows per week. Your first order of business is to train your instrument so that it is strong and supported by a healthy and reliable vocal technique.

Other CCM performers will need stamina, too, if they perform gigs of three or four sets a night, or long concert tours. Acquiring vocal training and practicing proper vocal exercise is the cornerstone of healthy vocal production that will serve the demands of your performing life.

Pitch

Even though *Vocal Fitness Training* emphasizes physical fitness for the voice, it still includes the musical aspects of vocal training, including singing accurate pitches. The vocal exercises consist of simple scales and melodic patterns, which develop pitch discipline by challenging the vocal cords to navigate specific vocal sequences.

Tone deafness is a common term that describes a condition in which a person has great difficulty matching pitch. There are certainly people who struggle with this and are in need of extensive work coordinating the neural, aural, and laryngeal movements. With the proper training, many can improve and learn to sing and match pitch, and there certainly is hope for many to overcome the challenge of tone deafness.

Training someone out of tone deafness is a huge undertaking, and it is beyond the scope of this book. However, if you are a singer who may struggle to stay in tune from time to time, it might be a result of your current vocal technique. The otherwise capable singer, with no apparent pitch-matching problems, will sometimes sing off key because they do not have the proper breath, muscle positions, or form to maintain pitch accuracy.

Once, I was attending a recording session for a student who was having trouble singing one pitch in tune. The producer, unhappy with the note, had him sing it several times without success. Frustrated, he turned to me and asked if I had any ideas. I went over to my student and after I adjusted his mouth position and breathing, he his sang his notes in tune and was able to move on to the next phrase.

In classical singing, performers regularly sing live in an acoustic environment where the absence of electronic amplification means that their pitch is not changeable through electronic means. Live, unamplified singing demands the highest level of pitch accuracy attained through intensive training, and it is rare to hear a professional opera singer described as being pitchy. Sure, occasionally an opera singer will sing a little sharp or flat, but they would never have made it in an opera career without a vocal technique that creates consistently accurate pitch. *Vocal Fitness Training's* exercises have their roots in traditional classical vocal technique, so training your voice in a similar manner will positively affect your ability to sing in tune.

Extending the Vocal Range

There certainly are limits to the ability of the human voice to produce measurable vocal pitch. However, many people are unaware that they have a larger vocal range than they are currently able to access. This happens for a number of reasons, but it is often just a function of inadequate vocal technique.

Since strong, flexible, and correctly positioned muscles give you better vocal tone, they will help improve your singing range. Also, remember that pitches are simply measured vibrations caused by the lengthening or shortening of the vocal cords. It makes sense that as your entire vocal instrument becomes more flexible, the vocal cords and the muscles in your larynx will be more adept at stretching and maintaining positions for pitches that are higher and lower than you were able to sing in the past. A reasonable long-term goal would be to expand your range so that you would be able to vocalize at least one whole step past the highest or lowest note that you would ever be called on to perform. That means that the highest or lowest note you would sing in public is not at the end of your workable vocal range. Of course, you can change any song into a different key, but your options might be limited if the original song spans a large range of notes, as *The Star-Spangled Banner* does.

As you work through this book, you may find that you do not know what the natural limits of your vocal range are until you have carefully trained your voice. The key is to work slowly and gently stretch those muscles through the specific skills and exercises presented here. *There is no quick fix for extending the vocal range*, even though the mechanics of the process are simple to learn. You cannot rush any training of the body, as it takes patience and practice to coordinate the new muscle movements to make a healthy and robust singing tone. This book focuses on creating a strong vocal foundation for further study of high notes in the future.

In My Studio

The physical movements of the human body to create sound involve many different muscle movements. Understanding the basic function of these movements will help you to understand the vocal exercises and to know how they assist with your vocal improvement.

Singers should be educated about the science side of their voices, but sometimes too much knowledge can be confusing. The material presented here is the same as that which I present to beginning students in this technique so that they will have grounding in the terminology and basic function of the vocal instrument. Please remember that vocal science is very helpful in explaining how the voice works, but not all of the science knowledge will have a direct application in the studio for teaching you how to sing. A well-designed, science-based vocal technique need not constantly rely on technical jargon to improve your singing. However, if you are so inclined and want to learn more about vocal science, there exist many resources beyond these pages.

THE NEXT STEP

Everything you have learned up to this point in the book gives you a solid intellectual foundation for proceeding with your vocal training. There are three things you need to remember and consider as you learn the rest of the material in this book:

- Vocal fitness is the goal. You want to approach the vocal exercises in the same manner as you would if you were going to the gym or a dance class. You will learn the proper movements and positions of your muscles and practice them until your body becomes accustomed to the movements. Over time, this will result in an automatic muscle memory of the positions needed to create a healthy sound and allow you to develop your acoustic resonance.

- Your articulators—the tongue, lips, and mouth—need to be in constant movement while producing your vocal tone. The exaggerated stretching will encourage this result, and as your muscles become more flexible and stronger, you will begin to experience a fluid stretching sensation as you sing from syllable to syllable. Any time you experience either locking or relaxation, you need to stop, restart your exercise, and ensure that you are in constant movement.

There is a section at the end of the book describing the components of transitioning from the exaggerated stretch to a more natural articulation, but your voice teacher or vocal coach should be the one to guide you through that adjustment. Until you reach that point, it will continue to be important for you to concentrate on strengthening the muscles and positions through practicing exaggerated stretch in the vocal exercises.

You may not experience the desired beautiful or perfect tone when you first begin the exercises. You must remain focused on the muscle positions and allow the voice to emerge on its own. This is especially true in the lower parts of your range. Resist the urge to push a loud sound out and instead replace that with a strong stretch. Your voice will gain volume on its own if you train it effectively. Remember that lower notes generally are lower in volume anyway, due to the lower frequencies in the sound waves.

CHAPTER 4
THE VOCAL EXERCISE TONE

The /oo/ vowel has the most forward lip position, and arguably it is the easiest exaggerated mouth position to learn first, as its shape is easy to achieve. This vowel will show you just how much you will need to work to increase strength and flexibility in the face and mouth and how those directly affect your vocal tone.

PRACTICAL VOCAL SCIENCE

Before you venture forward with your first singing exercise, you need to learn what type of vocal tone to produce while singing the exercises presented in *Vocal Fitness Training*'s materials. When you sing the exercises correctly, there will be a minimal amount of output of vibrato, resulting in what I describe as the *vocal exercise tone*. There is a reason for producing this type of simpler vocalization, so please take the time to read the next sections thoroughly before proceeding to the singing exercises.

Singing as Elongated Speech

If you have ever seen the musical *The Music Man*, you may recall that the lead character, Harold Hill, convinces four members of the town council to form a barbershop quartet by telling them that singing is simply nothing more than sustained speech, while aptly describing the commonality between singing and talking.

The primary difference between singing and speech, however, is that singing is a vocalization with the addition of specific pitch, duration, and volume. You can achieve duration as sustained vowel sounds, and in its purest form this tone is perceived to have very little to no vibrato. When you look at singing as an extension of speech, it becomes clear that we already have most of the tools to sing at our disposal. Our job is to learn how to enhance our speech patterns to the point where they become sustained, pitched tones.

Vibrato Defined

Vibrato is a perceived *slight* variation in pitch during tone production, and, when done well, it warms up the sound of the vocal tone. There are many different schools of thought on how to develop a vibrato, but the best and healthiest way is to let it occur naturally through the process of training your voice through a good vocal technique.

If you try to imitate, manufacture, or force muscles to create a vibrato effect, it can lead to problems such as jaw and tongue tension and has the potential to cause an uncontrolled vibrato. There are a few ways people make vibrato:

- Imitating what an opera singer sounds like by producing a big, wide wobbling sound.

- Approaching it as pitch variation, alternating between two pitches, steadily increasing the speed between them until achieving a vibrato effect.

- Manipulating the abdominal muscles by jerking them in and out.

- Relaxing the tongue and pushing the sound out from the larynx.

If you have heard of or learned any of these methods, realize that they are common approaches. The problem is that they often do not produce a vibrato that is a natural and free component of a healthy vocal tone as a result of a combination of proper articulation and breath management. Only after you have command of your vocal production can you expect the vibrato to emerge.

To do this, you first have to get your voice in shape, which begins with the vocal fitness exercises presented in this course. It will take time, but the rewards of a beautiful tone and healthy singing are well worth the effort. In order to get the best results from these vocal exercises, you should aim to sing them with the absence of an intentionally produced vibrato. As much as possible, avoid starting this new course with an incorrectly produced vibrato from either a relaxed or a manufactured approach.

However, it is extremely important for you to know that a *straight tone* is not what we want; that type of vocal tone may cause tension in the voice. For the purposes of our work here, we will call the tone we are seeking in these exercises the vocal exercise tone.

PRACTICAL EXERCISE PREPARATION

The Vocal Exercise Tone

Looking at the basics of vocal production, consider the idea that our voice functions similar to a wind instrument. For example, when the reed of a clarinet vibrates, it creates a fundamental pitch that travels through the hollow tube of the instrument. On its way, the acoustic properties of the interior of the clarinet enhance it and produce a basic tone, full of color but often with little to no apparent vibrato.

Our vocal instrument works similarly, but specific formations of the vocal tract are able to modify the sound before it leaves the mouth. Strong positioning of particular areas of the vocal tract creates the optimal acoustic space for the sound to pass through, after which it emerges naturally as a rich and healthy vocal tone. Although it may be without obvious vibrato, this tone contains warmth, color, and depth due to the presence of harmonic resonance.

Over time, and depending on your vocal style, a natural vibrato will emerge with this vocal exercise tone. It will be up to you, however, to determine how much or little vibrato you need for your singing style.

If you have come to this course with a relaxed vibrato, you will have to be especially vigilant with your strong, exaggerated articulation. The emphasis on stretching and strengthening the muscles to maintain a formation that encourages natural acoustic resonance will not allow you to relax to create a vibrato.

How to Assess Whether You Are Producing the Proper Vocal Exercise Tone

If you follow the instructions, are willing to make some silly faces to put your muscles into the proper position, and take time to breathe silently, you will begin to experience the production of a better vocal tone. If you are unsure if you are accomplishing this, try singing any exercise in the opposite manner, using a completely relaxed mouth, jaw, and tongue. Then sing it with the strong, exaggerated articulation. You should notice the difference, and the encouraging thing about this comparison is the more you practice and strengthen these movements, the more improvement you will see.

Lowering the Volume

Many students begin these exercises by singing them too loudly, especially in the lower range. There is a common misperception that one must "project" their voice to have it heard, which can result in the singer pushing from their throat. For example, when sung correctly, the exercise tone for the /oo/ and /oh/ vowels will have a quiet, and somewhat hooty or covered sound as heard from the inside. If you think you might be singing too loudly to either compensate for the quieter sound you are hearing internally, or are in the habit of pushing out your low notes, *cut your volume in half (or more) while maintaining the exaggerated stretch*. Although this may seem counterintuitive, it will allow the muscles to find new positioning, resulting in better vocal production overall. Once they are stronger, the acoustic resonance produced by the new internal positions will set up a more successful way to increase the volume.

You may recall that the focus of this course is on developing the low, medium, and medium-high areas of your voice to create a strong vocal foundation. *Only sing as far as you comfortably can in your range.* Do not feel that you have to sing every chord pattern presented in the exercise.

VOCAL IMAGERY: A HELPFUL TOOL

Vocal imagery is a tool that can assist you with moving muscles that you cannot see. You can coax the muscles into the proper position by relating their movement to a nonsinging position. For example, imagining certain shapes of food in the mouth, like a marshmallow to open up more space inside your mouth, can help you find the stretchy positioning of the muscles, instead of initiating vocal tension using some alternate means of awkward manipulation.

In the end, the goal of imagery is to keep you from overthinking direct muscular movement. Our bodies respond amazingly well to our thoughts, provided we have some sense of the image we are accessing. Images are useful for the short term, but eventually will give way to the muscle memory created by them. Think of them as helpful tools to get you started with the correct positions, encouraging and strengthening your vocal production.

IN MY STUDIO

I have had many students come to me with weak mouth and facial muscles. As odd as that may seem, it makes a lot of sense for those who have spent time singing in a relaxed manner. This happens because most people can make some type of reasonable singing tone without too much effort. Once they reach out for help and find out how to make the voice work efficiently, they realize that relaxed articulation hampers their ability to improve their singing.

There are many reasons for relaxed articulation, but often it is rooted in speech patterns. American English has many regional accents, and some of them are more laid-back, and they result in a slow and inactive articulation. As you work through this book, take a few minutes to assess your speaking voice. You may find that you are being held back by speaking one way and trying to sing in another way. Simply speaking with more energy in the articulation you learn here will help to bridge the gap between these two forms of vocal production.

All of the initial exercises in *Vocal Fitness Training* are for the medium and lower parts of your vocal range and are mixed and matched to give a complete workout throughout the week. Vocalizing on pitches nearer to your speaking voice allows you to more quickly understand and accomplish the goals set forth in each exercise.

The Practice Plans

Here are the essential guidelines for getting the most out of the Practice Plans:

- You can start any day of the week. To receive the most benefit from the Practice Plans, practice for six days before moving on. If you are following a shorter practice schedule (e.g., five days), simply practice the tracks on their indicated days.

- Practice daily, in the order listed, as the tracks are arranged in a specific sequence. Repeat each exercise a minimum of three times before moving to the next chord example. Think of this as the same as the reps you would do if you were lifting weights.

- Sing the exercises only as far in your range as is comfortable. Never force the sound, but allow your voice to improve naturally as you work it out over time.

- Practice all of the exercises in sequence on the given days, so you will get a variety of exercises that work out your voice and range.

- Always use a mirror to check your form and muscle movement.

- You are not limited to the exercises listed on any given day. You may add any other vocal exercise you have learned to your practice sessions.

- If you ever feel like you are having difficulty singing any of these exercises in the lower or higher part of your voice, such as experiencing tightening in the throat, stop immediately. The goal here is to exercise the muscles gently, and you have to give your body time to respond to the new tasks. Overworking the muscles to fatigue will be detrimental to your progress.

- The Practice Plan lists the exercise tracks in the order you will practice them. Remember to sing each example three times, in the same manner as you did in the lesson, checking your form in the mirror. Repeating the chord example multiple times is the same as the reps you would do if you were doing weight training at the gym. You need to create the muscle memory using the correct form to gain attain the desired results.

Corresponding Exercises, Practice Plans & Worksheets

The first set of exercises your teacher will introduce will correspond to everything you have read up to this point in the book. At the end of each lesson you will be given a Practice Plan to do, as well as a reading assignment and a worksheet. Later on, you will re-read some of the chapters and complete additional worksheets to reinforce the materials.

You may see additional Practice Plans at the VocalFitnessStudio.com website, but you should always do the one assigned by your teacher, as each is specific to the material you covered in your individual lesson. The extra plans are there for the readers of other editions of the Sing! books and may not apply to your learning that week. However, you certainly can use them for practicing in the future, once you have completed the basic training found in this book.

The exercises in the second half of this book are there to reinforce the instruction you receive from your teacher. They include step-by-step instructions, musical examples and helpful hints. Please take time to review this information after your lesson and before you begin your Practice Plans.

Here is the location of the exercises, and a list of the Practice Plans and worksheets that correspond to chapters 1-4:

The /oo/ vowel

Practice Plan Descriptions

Worksheet 1   Chapters 1-4

Worksheet 6   Chapter 3

Worksheet 7   Chapter 4

Worksheet 8   Chapter 3

All worksheets are available for download in the Member Download Library at VocalFitnessStudio.com

CHAPTER 5
PRACTICING STRATEGIES

This chapter introduces the information you need to know to practice effectively, and presents suggestions for successful self-teaching.

As you properly engage and balance your muscles, you will set up an acoustic environment that produces great vowel sounds. Singing is essentially sustained speech on pitch, with vowel sounds carrying most of that tone, and for that reason, every vocal exercise in this course, with the exception of humming, incorporates some type of vowel sound as its basis for strengthening the voice. Strong vowel production equals strong, beautiful, and healthy singing.

PRACTICAL EXERCISE PREPARATION

Intentional, thoughtful practicing generates new habits for healthy vocal production, and you will reap bigger benefits from this approach than if you practice mindlessly. Before you jump into your personal practice sessions, you will need to learn how to use a process known as *deliberate practicing*, which focuses on working in a slow and methodical manner.

How to Practice Effectively: Deliberate Practicing

Creating new muscle memory is a matter of refined repetition with the correct form. In order to cultivate new positions, you have to think about and tell your muscles how to move differently. This may make the practice sessions initially seem tedious, but the slow, deliberate approach reaps better results, as it forces you to redesign your muscle movements. Rapid, thoughtless practicing not only slows the improvement, but also reinforces incorrect positions.

For example, if you start an exercise track and sing each example one time without pausing to do the positions correctly, you are just going through the motions. This does not result in improved muscle movement because you have not taken the time to retool to the new position. It may also have the unfortunate result of reinforcing the old singing habits you are trying to change.

Instead, use the tools you have available to help monitor your movements, such as a mirror, and slowly practice each example a minimum of three times until you see some improvement.

Use Video Resources and Visual Feedback

Provided with all of the *Vocal Fitness Training* courses are links to demonstration videos that show the proper positions and muscle movements for the vocal exercises. This is a valuable tool to help you understand how to execute the new positions. Watching these videos after receiving instruction from your voice teacher or vocal coach can reinforce the concepts to help you further inform your practicing.

Additionally, visual feedback is a necessary component of vocal training, regardless of whether you are working with a teacher or not. When athletes are lifting weights at the gym, trainers will observe and correct their movements to promote both proper form and safety. Practicing vocal exercises is no different. You must take the time to check your progress visually, so you can assess, correct, and realign if necessary.

Many times in my studio, a student truly believes that they are moving their muscles correctly, but when they check themselves in a mirror, they see that they need to make an adjustment or correction to their vocal form or production. A mirror is an essential tool, and it is both inexpensive and portable. Similarly, if you have access to a video camera to record your lessons, it can give you both visual and aural feedback. People are now using their smartphones to video themselves during their practicing.

How to Listen to Your Voice to Facilitate Self-Teaching

Experience tells us that we do not actually hear our voices as they sound to others. How many times have you heard a recording of yourself (maybe as you are recording that perfect voice mail message), and you are very surprised at how you sound? Many people complain that it does not sound like them at all and even express dismay upon hearing their own voice!

To understand why this happens, consider that the sound waves you generate head away from you in the direction you are facing. Then, when they collide with an object, they bounce around, which means that it is rare that they would travel directly into your ear canal. Additionally, sound waves travel internally from your vocal cords as vibrations move to the inner ear through bone and tissue, adding yet another layer of internal sound to your hearing perception. When you add those internal and external sound waves together, it would appear that you are probably hearing yourself from more than one source, as well as with altered sounds. No wonder things sound different than we expect when we hear a recording of ourselves!

Can You Listen to Yourself?

When you start training your voice, you may perceive and hear some improvements from the inside, even though you are not hearing it as others do. However, despite this fact, there still are two ways to learn how to listen more accurately to the sound of your own voice: you can record yourself and listen back to it and you can learn how to interpret what you hear from inside your head.

However, you have to be careful because the biggest mistake people make when listening to themselves is trying to improve the sound they hear while they are singing. What they do not realize is that it is too late to correct a tone once it has left their mouth, and, more importantly, *their vocal production may not actually need correcting!*

When a singer attempts to correct their vocal sound by listening to their voice while singing, it often distracts them from focusing on the proper form, causing them to abandon the proper muscular movement or interfering with the changes they are working so hard to achieve. This is why most voice teachers correctly discourage their students from listening to themselves directly.

Ways to Listen Correctly

When you are in the process of learning how to listen to your own singing, you will need to observe how it both sounds *and* feels on the inside. Generally, the physical sensations of singing and the internal vibrations can give you good feedback. The key is to have a way to correlate those sensations and sounds you hear on the inside and determine whether they are correct.

There are a few ways to determine this, and the most important way is to have someone who can be your "ears." This will most likely be your voice teacher or vocal coach. You may also want to record yourself while practicing, or ask if you can record your voice lessons or coaching sessions. This kind of aural feedback can help you figure out what is working, and then you can use that knowledge to help you repeat the muscular movements that created a successful tone. Once you do develop a consistent, well-produced sound and become familiar with the internal sensations associated with it, you can listen to this *inside* voice to help guide you in your practicing.

There other things that can give you important feedback when singing the vocal exercises:

- If you think that your voice sounds quieter on the inside, it may surprise you to know that this may actually be a positive indicator of a new balance in the instrument, especially for those who have a history of pushing their voice, or oversinging. Some of the mouth positions we use, such as for the vowel /oo/, may produce this type of quieter result. Avoid trying to adjust the volume louder to compensate for what you may perceive as a tone that is too small. The goal is to exercise the muscles and produce new muscle memory, and the sound and volume will improve in time.

- This book focuses on strengthening the middle and lower voice, which naturally creates vocal tone at a lower volume. Remember to stay focused on

- changing muscle movement, and the acoustic properties you are creating will eventually give you the amount of sound you need.

- You might feel as if your throat is opening up, or it might feel more relaxed than before. That can be a good sign, provided you use the strong, exaggerated articulations properly. If so, the feeling of an open throat would indicate the absence of previous tension. Be careful, though, as the goal is never to relax the throat—the goal is never to relax anything, for that matter—because a solid vocal technique results in balanced muscle movement.

Digital Recording and Listening

In this age of digital everything, recording devices are available on smartphones, tablets, computers, and as stand-alone devices. The primary key to a good recording for your practicing, however, is the quality of both the microphone and the playback equipment. If you are relying on a recording device to give you accurate feedback, the process has to reflect the sounds you are making. If you use a built-in microphone, like those on smartphones, you may not end up with the quality of recording you need. In addition, once you have a good recording, you must play it through good-quality speakers or headphones to hear the most accurate details and nuances of your vocal production.

A handheld digital recorder is my favorite recording device because it is very portable. In my experience, recorders that retail around $75 or more usually have a decent enough built-in microphone to prevent your voice from overdriving and distorting the recording with white noise. Another option is to purchase a less expensive recorder with an external port and connect a microphone to that.

Alternatively, you could use recording software on your computer, but you will still need a decent microphone and easy access to your computer when practicing. There are a few good-quality microphones on the market that plug into some smartphones and tablets, but I do not have any personal experience with those products. In the end, the test is simply going to be if the combination of recording software, microphone choice, and playback equipment will give you an accurate representation of your voice.

One thing to be aware of is that your microphone placement can make a difference in the quality of your recording. Once you get your recording gear set up, record a sample vocal with the microphone at five different distances. Depending on your equipment, you will likely get five different results. Listen back and determine how far away you should be from the microphone to get the best representation of your voice. Then consistently place the microphone in that position.

Also, keep in mind that audio recordings take up a lot of digital space, so make sure the recording device you use has enough storage capacity or has the ability to save to expandable media such as a flash drive or SD card.

Should You Go for the Burn? Never!

The goal is to strengthen the muscles with daily practice just like a workout at the gym. Unlike traditional workouts though, we are not overloading the muscles to failure in order to strengthen them. However, it is not unusual if you sometime feel a little fatigue in the facial muscles or tongue, and therefore you should limit your practice sessions initially to between ten and fifteen minutes at a time.

When you increase the length of your practice sessions, you might want to consider splitting your time up into smaller increments with a *vocal time-out* in between. You take a vocal time-out by ceasing to make any sounds for ten to fifteen minutes. This means that you will not talk, laugh, sing, whisper, or make any kind of sound with your vocal cords. This will give your voice a nice little break before you return to your singing practice.

A short, focused workout also provides the time for you to execute the exercises correctly but does not overtax the muscles or vocal cords. Please remember that this approach of strong, exaggerated articulation allows the throat, vocal cords, and their attendant muscles to operate freely and in balance with each other.

When you practice, sing the exercises only as far in your range as is comfortable, and do not force a note in order to finish the exercise track (or to prove to yourself that you can). If you push beyond what you are *currently* capable of doing, you will negatively force the vocal cords to produce sound. As your muscles become stronger and more flexible, the exaggerated stretching will begin to open up other areas of your range.

The primary goals are to stretch your articulatory muscles gently to encourage the new, proper form and to strengthen the muscles that manage vocal production to help them gain flexibility, endurance, and new muscle memory. However, as with any physical exercise you must start slowly and make sure you are doing the movements properly and consistently.

As with any physical endeavor, your skills will improve with practice. Similar to working out at the gym, the correct form is necessary to create new habits and muscle memory. Remember that intentional, thoughtful practicing reaps bigger benefits than just going through the motions.

In My Studio

Every once in a while, I will have a student whose improvement slows down a bit. Since improvement is contingent on practicing, I will ask the student about his or her particular practice schedule, and sometimes I get a very interesting answer:

"I'm practicing my exercises... in the car... while I'm loading the dishwasher... while walking the dog." The excuse for practicing in these environments is a lack of time, so they say that they are trying to fit in their vocal practice here and there.

This simply does not work! If you want to change the way your muscles move, you have to spend time working them in the positions needed for better vocal production. At the very least, you have to use a mirror to receive visual feedback, and that is a downright dangerous thing while you are driving a car! You also should either stand or sit up in a correct posture during vocal practicing. None of this is possible if you practice in a car, or in a kitchen, or in a tree, or in a box! So please do not cheat yourself out of real improvement by thinking that vocal practicing is something you do only when you have the time. Set aside daily practice time in an appropriate space to work on your voice so you can give yourself a real opportunity to improve your singing. And, please remember this: Anyone can find fifteen minutes a day to practice vocal exercises.

The Next Step

The exercises are progressive by design, to strengthen and build your voice, so your improvement is dependent on doing the exercises in the order presented in the course. Learning the exaggerated articulation can be challenging for some, as it can depend on how much mouth and facial movement you were doing prior to beginning the exercises. If you had a relaxed vocal technique, it could take you a few weeks to get the muscle strength to move forward to the next group of exercises.

CHAPTER 6
THE VOWEL /OH/ AND SIMPLE BREATHING

The first exercises you learned emphasize the articulation component of vocal production. Breath management is the other important factor that enriches the tone, and later chapters will discuss that further. In the meantime, strong, exaggerated articulation tends to induce enough air to create a natural tone that is useful for practicing. However, this is a good time to begin incorporating two simple breathing strategies with the practice song, "How Can I Keep from Singing?"

PRACTICAL VOCAL SCIENCE
The Closed /oh/ Pronunciation

The vowel sound /oh/ used in the vocal exercises is considered a *closed sound* because of its exaggerated forward position. This can be somewhat challenging for American English speakers in particular, as the familiar "oh" sound tends to be less forward, or in some cases, does not occur at all. Since we are changing our vocal habits for singing, you might initially struggle with the over exaggerated, unfamiliar shape necessary for this closed /oh/ vowel sound.

You may wonder why we would choose to sing a vowel sound that is more common in other languages such as French, German, or Italian. Proper exaggerated pronunciation of the closed /oh/ stretches the interior and exterior muscles and aids in the strengthening and flexibility of the mouth. After you have gained mastery over this vowel position and gained flexibility in the muscle movements, you will not need the extreme exaggeration, as it eventually gives way to a more natural articulation and shape.

EXERCISE PREPARATION
Finding the /oh/ Position

A great way to find the /oh/ position is to relate it to the similar articulation produced by the /oo/ vowel. Alternating between these two vowels produces a slight change in the opening of your lips as space opens up inside of your mouth while your jaw drops slightly downward to accommodate this more open vowel. In the low range, the lips form a circular shape and size similar to the /oo/, but the inside of the mouth retains an open shape.

Also, many of the /oh/ exercises use the vowel and consonant-sound combination /yoh/. As with the /yoo/ exercises, linger for a moment as you begin to sing the "y" sound and then glide into the /oh/. This engages the tongue as you keep the energy going while you transfer the movement from the tongue to the lips.

Stop Gaspy Breathing

Some singers make an audible gasping sound when they breathe for singing. As a rule, these gaspy breaths are noisy, indicate shallow breathing, and cause a lower intake of air into the lungs. However, when you breathe silently, it initiates a deeper breath that expands the ribs and secures more air in the lungs to initiate vocal cord vibration. At first, you may notice that the silent intake may seem to slow your inhalation, but that is the short-term result, as it gives you more air to work with for your practicing.

Breathe Early, Breathe Often

In order to create good vocal tone, and to keep your voice healthy, you must learn to breathe *before* you have used up too much air. Using this method refills the lungs so that you can benefit from singing on a cushion of residual air. To make this a habit, you must learn to *breathe early* and *breathe often*. This may seem counterintuitive, but over time, this sipping of the breath actually strengthens and coordinates the breath by teaching your body how to manage the vocal tone on a small, but consistent stream of compressed air.

You can also gain from thoughtful breathing throughout the day while speaking by practicing the silent inhalation and the strategy of *breathe early, breathe often*. This will help you to develop the awareness and experience of deep inhalation and rib-cage movement.

IN MY STUDIO

My students will often ask me how they should warm up their voices. The answer is simple, use vocal exercises! When students cannot warm up before their lessons, I turn to a five to seven-minute warm-up routine that primarily uses Exercise 7D, the connected /yoo/, and Exercise 18A, the connected /yoh/. They are excellent when you need to get things moving a bit before a rehearsal or voice lesson.

Generally, I recommend singing the /yoo/ exercises (Exercise 7D) first, on a descending track, to warm up the low notes. After that, switch to the /yoh/ syllable (Exercise 18A), and sing up into the medium-high range. Regardless of what exercises you choose as a warm-up, they should be gently progressive.

Orbicularis Oris Accessing the Forward Stretch

Many muscles assist in the forward movement of the lips, and one of the most helpful is the *orbicularis oris*, which encircles your lips. This muscle helps to bring your lips into the forward positions of both the /yoo/ and /yoh/ syllables and helps to strengthen the articulation of these vowels.

Just for fun, say the name of this muscle aloud a few times, running the two Latin words together: orbicularis oris. You may notice that it now sounds like the name of a dinosaur—the "orbicularisaurus." Although silly, it is an effective way to remember the name of this muscle and its role in exaggerated articulation!

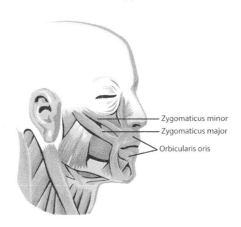

Zygomaticus minor
Zygomaticus major
Orbicularis oris

THE NEXT STEP

There are no shortcuts to good vocal technique. Remember, having reliable singing skills is not just about good tone, but how they assist you with vocal health and developing a strong instrument that has the stamina to sing the kinds of music you enjoy. Take your time and follow the guidance of your voice teacher or vocal coach to make sure you are devoting adequate time to learning and integrating these new muscle movements and concepts.

CORRESPONDING EXERCISES, PRACTICE PLANS & WORKSHEETS

Here are the exercises, Practice Plans, and worksheet for chapters 5-6:

The /oh/ vowel

Practice Plan Descriptions

Worksheet 2 Chapters 5 & 6

Available in the Member Download Library at VocalFitnessStudio.com

CHAPTER 7

THE VOCAL CRY

Singing, by definition, demands a sustained vocalization on pitch. Since vowel sounds are the primary carriers of pitch, you want to both strengthen and coordinate the articulation of the vowel with pitch. This exercise teaches the vocal cords to smoothly transition from fast vibrations of a higher note to slow vibrations of a lower tone, all the while sustaining vocal tone.

You will do this by elongating the /oo/ vowel sound with a technique called the *cry*. To sing a cry, you will begin singing on a specific pitch, and glissando or glide slowly through a group of nonspecific pitches, similar to the sound you would hear produced by a siren, owl, or slide whistle. The goal is to produce as many pitches as possible between the five notes of the cry and use the stretching muscles of articulation to maintain the acoustic-resonance space.

PRACTICAL VOCAL SCIENCE

There are a number of vocal training terms floating around that mean different things to different people. The term *cry* is no exception. In this book, we will use it to describe the siren-style glissando taught for many years in vocal studios. There are other terms for this glissando vocalization, and there are other definitions of the word *cry* used in vocal pedagogy. *For the purposes of this book, we will use* cry *to mean a sustained glissando produced between a series of pitches.*

Cries are, at their heart, a combination of elongated speech and easy calling, as in the phrases "Hey, wait! Wait for me! Wait up!" Be careful and do not confuse this with your screaming or shouting voice, or the commonly heard vocalized sigh. When sung properly, cries are not loud, instead, they are produced with a gentle stretch that releases the voice, allowing it to "cry out." The goal when singing cries is to achieve the most consistent glide through the pitches and to maintain the beauty of tone.

There are numerous examples available of cries, and I strongly urge you to use the exercise tracks to help you learn how to make the best cry possible. Mimicking the sound will be very helpful as long as you are careful to maintain the correct articulation positions. I highly recommend drawing on your inner child and making some fire truck siren sounds, as they are a great example of the vocalization you need to sing a cry! The cry stretches all of the muscles of the vocal apparatus in concert as it navigates the different pitches in your voice. In many exercises, the cry will cross from one register to another, helping the muscles to become more flexible and balanced.

As your cries improve, you may begin to notice that you will have smoother shifting in the areas of the register changes. Cries also challenge the breath, as sustained sound requires a steady column of air to continue producing the sound properly.

BELTING AND THE CRY

In both popular music and in some musical theater styles there is vocal production called *belting*. Simply put, singers use specific muscles in the larynx to produce a stronger sound up through the vocal range. It is important for singers who use this style of singing to make sure they receive the proper training, because if learned improperly this can cause a great deal of tension, fatigue, and potential damage.

Belt training per se is not within these pages, but learning how to execute the cry exercises properly in this chapter can help you strengthen and prepare your voice to undertake the more demanding vocalizations such as belting. The simple belt-like sound created through all the vocal cry exercises can help you develop healthy vocal production and teach you how to navigate the part of your range that uses the belt. A strong vocal cry is a very good foundation for the belt sound, and it is worth investing the time to learn its production.

IN MY STUDIO

Without question, cry exercises are a studio favorite, and my students often beg to do them in their lessons! It brings out the little kid in everyone, especially with the playful siren-like quality of the exercise. Students find that the cries show them how they can harness the acoustic power of the instrument and how the exaggerated stretch can develop a stronger tone. It may not be apparent at first, but the cry exercises will become a cornerstone of your vocal technique, as they help to keep you rooted firmly in the vocal exercise tone.

Cries in the high range are a great game changer when developing that part of your voice, but they demand a specific instruction sequence and practice regimen. Since vocal study in this book focuses on developing and strengthening the low and medium voice, I would highly discourage you from venturing into the higher range with the cries until you have reached a level of competency and vocal strength, and your voice teacher or vocal coach feels you are ready. Instruction modules will be available at VocalFitnessStudio.com for you and your teacher after you have completed this course, that will explore further the instruction and methods for learning how to sing upper range cries properly and successfully.

The Next Step

Chapter 8 will take you in a completely new direction as it introduces breathing for singing. Up to this point, the emphasis has been on developing and enhancing the acoustic resonator space in your vocal tract, with only minimal breathing instruction: inhale silently and *breathe early, breathe often*. If you are wondering why, there is a simple answer. The body knows how to produce just enough breath to learn the concepts of strong, exaggerated speech and singing articulation, and that is fine for learning this vocal technique in the low and middle voice. Therefore, *Vocal Fitness Training* takes the initial steps to strengthen the articulation and tone production first, *before* exploring the significant area of breathing for singing.

Corresponding Exercises, Practice Plans & Worksheets

Here are the exercises, Practice Plans, and worksheets for chapter 8:

The Vocal Cry

Practice Plan Descriptions

Worksheet 4

Available in the Member Download Library at VocalFitnessStudio.com

CHAPTER 8
BREATHING TO SING

This chapter focuses on learning the basics of the respiratory system as it relates to breathing for singing, as well as acquiring skills to begin to access and execute the breathing functions necessary for success with breath management.

The manner in which a singer both takes in and manages their breath is crucial to the success of the vocal sound. This chapter has a specific approach, because the goal is to learn how to enhance and manage the breath in an effective, efficient way, to allow the vocal cords to vibrate freely. Every singer must have a basic knowledge of the respiratory process in conjunction with the practice of well-constructed vocal exercises to strengthen and integrate the breathing with the vocal production.

PRACTICAL VOCAL SCIENCE
Breathing for Singing

Many singers are unfamiliar with good breathing strategies or have experienced breathing instruction that is sketchy or confusing. On the other hand, there are singers who are fortunate enough to have well-informed teachers who completely understand the breathing mechanism and successfully train them. The breath management approach presented here is a result of my own personal journey of work with former teachers, colleagues, study, and research. I have drawn primarily from the ideas put forth in schools of classical vocal pedagogy that tap into the use of compressed breath. However, I would prefer to avoid labeling this *breathing instruction;* it is just a strategy to learn how to manage breathing for singing effectively.

The approach is to start slowly and build on your knowledge and awareness of how to use the breath for singing. Once you become aware of the feelings within your body that occur when the breath is taken in and let out, then you can learn how to coordinate that with the singing process. *Vocal Fitness Training's* materials are purposefully progressive, so as you become more adept with your breathing skills, additional vocal exercises will challenge both your voice and breath further.

Breath Management

Here is why the breath is so important:

1. Without air, there is no sound from the vocal cords.

2. Without continuous air, there is no sustained sound.

3. Without sustained sound, there is no singing.

4. To sing well, you need to find a method to keep the air flowing unimpeded

5. through the vocal cords.

Simple logic might dictate that you should take in as much air as possible and hope that this big breath keeps the tone flowing to the end of the phrase. Inevitably, though, this approach will cause you to run out of breath, gasping for air as your body attempts to refuel its oxygen needs. A gasping cycle like this results in an ongoing shortness of breath and robs the tone of its strength and color.

Another approach to breath management might be to interfere with the work of the abdominal muscles in an attempt to slow down exhalation and the natural recoil of the diaphragm. Although a valid idea, the problem with this approach is that it can sometimes cause a singer to clench the abdominal muscles incorrectly and tighten them to the point where they lock up the entire breathing process.

To find a way to manage your breath for singing, you have to understand the process by which the vocal cords initiate the fundamental sound. Although the following example appears to be in consecutive steps, most of this happens so quickly that it almost seems simultaneous:

1. You breathe in and fill up your lungs with more air than you would need for common speech.

2. The brain sends a signal to tell the vocal cords to come together as a response to wanting to vocalize.

3. As exhalation begins, air pressure builds up under the closed vocal cords until

4. they are blown apart, initiating the first vibration.

5. The vocal cords return to their original position, then open and close again, repeating this cycle many times per second, creating vocal sound or pitch.

Considering that air pressure provides the energy that starts the onset the vocal of sound, it follows that it would have to be a primary factor in understanding breath management. Therefore, before we even think of trying to harness or mechanically control the release of the breath, we first need to prepare an environment where we can accumulate a reasonable amount of compressed air in the lungs to initiate and sustain a singing tone.

The Balloon

Let us look at how compressed air works by examining what happens when you blow up a balloon and make it squeak by pulling on its neck. The balloon squeaks as long as there is enough compressed air traveling across the stretched opening in the neck of the balloon. As the air pressure decreases inside, the speed and energy of the air slows and the squeaking stops, although the balloon may still appear to have a fair amount of air in it. The squeaking subsides because the remaining air simply is too weak to continue producing sound.

A similar situation can occur in vocal production if a singer releases too much air or completely runs out of breath while singing. When the residual air in the lungs decreases too much to sustain the vocal tone, it will stop completely.

EXERCISE PREPARATION

The Concept of Using Compressed Air for Singing

Imagine that you have a reservoir of air in your lungs that feeds your vocal sounds at a constant rate and pressure. This is what happens when a singer learns how to harness the energy of the breath through a concept referred to as *compressed air*. Here's how to get started:

1. Fill your lungs with the proper amount of air.

2. Begin to sing a few notes or a short phrase.

3. Without releasing the air left in your lungs, refill the breath that you used up.

4. Sing.

5. Repeat steps 3 and 4 until you have finished the song.

When you approach your breathing for singing this way, you breathe *before* you have used up the entire volume of air in your lungs, which effectively creates a reserve of air upon which you can sing. You encountered this concept, *breathe early, breathe often*, for the first time in Exercise 15. However, to execute this breathing strategy successfully, you must first gain a complete understanding and sense of what it feels like to expand your ribs and determine how to fill your lungs with a proper amount of compressed air.

Using Compressed Air Efficiently and Effectively

We can see that a good reservoir of air will assist with the onset of vocal tone, but that is not the end of the story. You must not exhale too much air too quickly or sing to the end of your breath. When your body senses a lack of oxygen, it will work quickly to get air back into the body with a sudden inhalation, generally manifesting as a shallow or gasping breath. This type of quick breath is ineffective for singing because it immediately disrupts the ability to breathe in the adequate amount of air needed to set up an environment of compressed air in the lungs.

Another negative effect caused by gasping is called *gripping*. With the absence of adequate air pressure to produce sound effortlessly with the vocal cords, the body turns to muscles adjacent to the larynx for help. If you have ever had your throat tighten up (and hurt) while singing, you have likely experienced this gripping effect. Over time the stress on the throat from gripping can contribute to a myriad of more serious vocal problems (often referred to as *phonotrauma)* such as nodules, polyps, or even vocal cord hemorrhage.

Although you may be able to continue to produce vocal sound, you should never put yourself in the position where you are singing at any cost, as it can severely push the instrument out of balance. Gasping and gripping are probably the most common vocal production problems related to breathing, and they can very quickly stress the vocal instrument and cause fatigue. The long-term goal is to learn to replace these habits with a more comprehensive strategy of using compressed breath to enable the vocal cords to vibrate with as little effort as possible and to create a healthy vocal tone with a steady flow of air.

DISCOVERING THE INTERCOSTAL MUSCLES

There are many interrelated respiratory muscles working together to help us breathe all day long. The intercostal muscles, which are located on the interior and exterior of the ribs, help to expand and contract the ribs when you breathe, moving them into the proper position during these processes.

When you inhale, the ribs expand laterally as the diaphragm contracts down, drawing air into the lungs and increasing the size of the thoracic cavity. Our goal is to become aware of the movement of the intercostal muscles and the ribs, to assist in our understanding of expanding our lung capacity while singing.

Lung Capacity

Breathing for singing is easier to understand when you acquire some technical knowledge to help you understand the volume and capacity of the lungs. Actual lung volume and capacity varies widely from person to person, but to simplify the following discussion and explanations, we will use average numbers for the examples.

At rest, both lungs can contain an average volume of approximately two liters of air, which increases by about one-half liter when inhaling. However, the maximum average amount a person can inhale is around six liters, or almost three times that resting amount!

Six liters of air (or completely full) would be an excessive amount of air from which to sing, as it would create too much pressure underneath the vocal cords, be difficult to control, and feel quite uncomfortable. However, if you were to breathe halfway, it would feel like not quite enough air, so we need to find that point somewhere between halfway and full, where there is enough air to correctly initiate and sustain vocal sound without overfilling.

The following chart shows basic lung-capacity and lung-volume information that you need to become familiar with in order to understand the functioning of the lungs as it relates to breathing for singing. Each level of inhalation has a simple description followed by its scientific label.

Please take some time to study this chart, as the concepts are critical to the understanding of breathing for singing, and we will base our discussion of breathing going forward on these lung-capacity examples. This is probably the most technical chart in the book, but it will help you to understand the basics of how the breath functions in the human body and how you can use that knowledge to improve your breathing for singing.

As you study the *Inspiratory Reserve Volume* section in the chart below, you will notice a reference to *position five* or *breathing to five*. This is the desired comfortably full position, where you have enough air in your lungs to create an environment of compressed air but they are not so completely full that it is uncomfortable. Please understand that we are not interested in determining the actual amount of air in your lungs by scientific calculation and measurement but rather helping you to discover the sensation of increasing your lung capacity to a position that gives you a foundation for effective and efficient breathing.

Exercise 24 will help you explore the sensation of finding the inhalation position called *six*, so you may gain a solid understanding of the capacity of your own lungs at their fullest. Later, you will learn two processes to help you determine position five. Once you have found position five, we will use that term to describe the minimal amount of air needed to begin singing and simply call that breathing to five.

Approximate Number of Liters	Description of Lung Volumes	Description of Lung Capacity
1 2	**Residual Volume:** the amount of air that remains in the lungs keeping them from collapsing. **Expiratory Reserve Volume:** an additional amount of residual air that does not deplete all of the air in your lungs as you exhale.	**Functional Residual Capacity:** The sum of the two categories (at left). We will refer to this total capacity as the average of *Two* liters of air always present in our lungs.
2.5	**Tidal Volume:** the amount of air that we breathe in and out at rest, over and above the residual air capacity that remains in our lungs (see 1 and 2 above). For the average person, it amounts to approximately .5 liters.	
3 4 5 6	**Inspiratory Reserve Volume:** this is the additional capacity over the tidal volume (see 2.5 above). We will tap into this additional lung capacity to breathe in the extra air we need for singing. We do not want to fill up completely, but target a *comfortably full* feeling which we call *position five*. We will refer to this as *position five or breathing to five*. The numbers to the left indicate the approximate additional inhaled liters of air possible.	**Inspiratory Capacity:** The total volume of additional inhaled air. We will refer to this as *Breathing to Six*, as it is the total average amount of capacity available.

The Diaphragm and Abdominal Muscles

The diaphragm is a dome-shaped muscle that stretches horizontally across the body. At rest, it looks a bit like a parachute, with its center resting just below the heart and lungs. Its primary function is to regulate inhalation, and when it contracts it flattens a bit and descends, creating a vacuum in the thoracic cavity that draws air into the lungs (inhalation). Then it releases, returning to its original position as air leaves the lungs (exhalation).

You may hear people say we can control the diaphragm directly to influence its movement, using the common phrase "support with your diaphragm." Although the diaphragm's role in breathing for singing is significant, efficient breathing is not the perceived manipulation of this muscle. Still, we can learn to correctly balance other muscles that are in close relation to the diaphragm that will influence its movement. However, any attempt to do this before attaining basic breathing skills can have a negative effect by causing unwanted tension. Therefore, you can "support with the diaphragm" or "lean on the breath" as much as you like, but until you are proficient at filling the lungs with sufficient air, you will not have any breath to manage.

Respiration

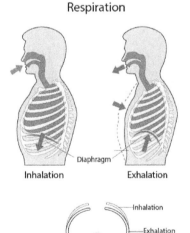

Inhalation   Diaphragm   Exhalation

Inhalation
Exhalation

Position of the ribs during
inhalation and exhaltion

BREATHING TO FIVE VS. QUICKER BREATHS

You may start to feel that you are not inhaling exactly to position five on the quicker breaths, and that is okay. The goal is to start to feel how easily breath returns to your lungs when you do not collapse and release the air. Remember, position five is being comfortably full of air. At this point in your breathing study, you need to acquire an awareness of the breath, as well as exercising and coordinating the muscles involved in the process.

Performing and the New Breathing Skills

If you are performing regularly, do not worry about integrating all of these new breathing skills into your songs quite yet. Practice the breathing technique when singing the vocal exercises for now. In the meantime, there are a few small things you can do in this transitional phase of learning how to breathe more efficiently for singing:

1. Breathe to five at the beginning of a phrase and when you have a break in the music.

2. From now on, avoid singing to the end of your breath. Go through your songs and map out where you are going to take breaths, using the concept of *breathe early, breathe often*, and practice them with these intentional, planned breaths.

3. Avoid taking a gaspy breath at all costs! If you can hear yourself take in air, you are gasping. Breathing silently will yield better breath pressure, exercise your breathing muscles, improve your tone, and help your vocal cords to vibrate efficiently.

In addition to practicing your vocal exercises by breathing to five, you will need to start the process of analyzing the songs you sing to determine where you can fit in extra breaths. Do not worry about whether or not you can sing a certain phrase in one breath. That will come in time, and, as strange as this sounds, the best way to develop the ability to sing longer lines in one breath, is to practice breathing more often within a song.

When you solidify the connection between the vocal onset and the breath, it strengthens the muscle coordination within the context of singing. Interestingly enough, an audience will barely hear the extra quick breaths you take because those breaths will be small and silent, but they probably will notice it if you run out of breath.

Breathing Skills Take Time

The most important thing for you to remember is that it takes time to master the management of breathing for singing. This chapter is just the starting point of understanding and creating better coordination and muscle memory, and you cannot rush this step.

Please take the time to fully understand and integrate these foundational concepts, as they will serve you well as you improve and add other challenges to your breathing training. This book will take you to the point where the vocal exercises will work in tandem with breath-management strategies to strengthen and coordinate muscle movement. However, you must focus on breathing from now on; every time you open your mouth to sing you will have to think about breath. Certainly, you could sing without all of this special attention to breathing, but to ignore it would be doing a disservice to your voice and will hinder your improvement and vocal tone.

In My Studio

Once I had a student who was struggling with some breathiness in her voice. Unbeknownst to me, she was also having upper back issues. She made an appointment to see her chiropractor to get some relief, and when she came for a voice lesson the next day, the breathiness was almost completely gone! The tension in her upper back muscles had apparently transferred into the larynx, causing poor vocal tone. She continued her treatment and retained the clarity in her singing. This is a dramatic story, but the lesson learned here is that good posture promotes balance throughout the upper body, which is needed for the breath and to free up all the muscles involved in vocal production. You may not have to visit a doctor to release your muscles, but paying attention to your posture can make a huge difference.

The Next Step

Develop Basic Breathing Skills First

Later in this book, you'll learn more about how to improve and advance the execution of the breathing technique. You must completely understand and practice the first steps presented in this chapter before proceeding with other breathing instruction in this course because your goal is to retrain the muscle movements and develop coordination while singing.

Breathing for singing is unlike any other type of respiratory activity, and patience and tenacity are the keys that will lead you to better breath management. Keep in mind that it is well worth your time to acquire the basic skills of breathing to five and the strategy of *breathe early, breathe often.*

THE BREATHING FOR SINGING TOP TEN LIST

10. Using compressed air to sing helps to keep the vocal tone free and clear.

9. Avoiding noisy, gaspy breaths increases the volume of air drawn into your lungs.

8. One must practice breathing while singing, in both exercises and songs.

7. Posture is vital!

6. Intercostal muscles expand the rib cage and help to draw more air deeply into the lungs.

5. Understanding that the lungs have great capacity helps us to understand that there is a large reservoir of air available to tap into and leverage as compressed air.

4. Determining the comfortably full position using the concept of breathing to five takes time, but it reveals the concept of how to use compressed air to sing.

3. After you finish inhaling, avoid holding your breath before you sing, and instead sing on the outflow of air.

2. When practicing, remember to *breathe early, breathe often*, to teach your body how to manage the flow of air.

1. Allow your body the time it needs to learn how to integrate the movements by practicing them slowly and thoughtfully.

CORRESPONDING EXERCISES, PRACTICE PLANS & WORKSHEETS

Here are the exercises, Practice Plans, and worksheets for chapter 8:

Breathing to Sing

Practice Plan Descriptions

Worksheets 3 and 5
Available in the Member Download Library at VocalFitnessStudio.com

CHAPTER 9

Humming and the /ee/ Vowel

Some singers use a lifted, smiling position as a way to improve their vocal production because there is a sense that doing so lifts the palate, creating better acoustic-resonance space in the back of the mouth. Smiling does seem to have some positive effects there, which makes it a worthwhile tool for short-term vocal training. On the other hand, a total smiling approach does have detractors because of its seemingly artificial position and tendency toward locking. If one understands the reason behind using a smiling position and learns when it is and is not an appropriate way to train the voice, it can prove to be a very helpful way to improve vocal tone.

We will discuss two distinct types of humming and introduce the concept and application of the natural smiley stretch in the production of the primary vowel sound /ee/ (as in *fleece*).

Practical Vocal Science

The Natural Smiley Stretch: A Short-Term Vocal Tool

At one point during my vocal study, I was encouraged to use a smiling position throughout my range on many vowels. Unfortunately, overuse of this position caused my upper range to become strident and shrill, and it took some different training, and serious practicing, to erase those unfortunate habits. To be clear, any use of a smiling position from here forward is a short-term strategy to strengthen muscle articulation and flexibility in the middle and low ranges only. Eventually, it will give way to less exaggeration.

The primary goals for using a natural smiley stretch are to influence internal articulation and to create a better acoustic-resonance space inside the mouth. Over time, there will be less need for the extreme outward facial stretch of the smile position, as the vowel production will settle naturally into position when there is a release of the exaggeration. The muscles will become stronger and more flexible, and all you will need is a slight lift both on the inside and outside along with the internal stretch to maintain this acoustic space.

Interestingly, the natural smiley stretch can be a great asset for singing in the very low ends of the range, as it can help prevent you from bearing down on the vocal cords to crank out the heavy low notes. Using a natural smiley stretch can sometimes make a difference in whether or not the pitch will actually occur. You may find that you will call on this exaggerated stretch from time to time in this lower part of your range.

EXERCISE PREPARATION

Finding the Natural Smiley Stretch

The way to find the proper position for the natural smiley stretch is to laugh. Laughing engages the eyes, which in turn engages the facial muscles and creates a meaningful stretch. he natural smiley stretch should never be forced or locked onto your face. When done properly, it will feel like a cheerful, continuous stretch. Here are a few things you can think of to initiate this position:

- Imagine you are smiling to your ears.

- Imagine the stretch begins at the bottom of your cheeks and moves on an angle toward your ears.

- Tell yourself a corny joke!

Humming

Humming is a vocal exercise that is easy to do and good for the voice. The key is to execute the hum properly so it both engages and balances the breath with the vocal cords. The hum is very helpful for jump-starting vowels like /ee/ or /ah/, as it naturally contains the consonant sound "m," which assists in setting up strong vibration and resonance.

Humming with a strong, natural smiley stretch will make you aware of the natural vibration in the upper acoustic regions of your face, and it will nudge the inside of your mouth into position for a good vowel tone.

To find the proper mouth position for strong humming, you will begin with the sound "hnn." As you first learn this position for the hum, it is okay to preset the natural smiley stretch before you breathe. When your muscles are a little stronger, you will need to stop presetting and learn to initiate the smile and hum simultaneously.

Relaxed Humming

Although most of the training in this vocal technique stresses the strong, exaggerated articulation in the mouth, relaxed humming uses a mouth position that is not exaggerated, and it is an ideal vocalization strategy for warming up a cold voice.

The key to creating a relaxed hum is to let the voice naturally vibrate and to allow any register changes to occur without trying to manipulate them. It is best done in mid to low range, but some higher voices have great success humming well into their upper range. Although the actual articulation in your mouth is intentionally relaxed, you will still need to pay careful attention to your breathing when singing a relaxed hum. There are no exercises for this humming example, as it simply entails humming with a relaxed mouth and tongue. A relaxed humming exercise in this course is only used as a tool for warming up or warming down the voice.

In My Studio

New students that enter my studio are unfamiliar with the idea of engaging their facial muscles to sing. Therefore, they often find it difficult to challenge those muscles in the activities of external stretching, at first. The /ee/ vowel is the most challenging, due to the exaggerated smiley stretch of the cheek muscles. It takes some practicing to get those muscles loosened up and moving in the right direction. However, you need to learn how to articulate this vowel correctly, because it has the strongest articulation position of the vowels pronounced with a natural smiley stretch. A well-produced, properly executed /ee/ vowel will help you when you learn the other stretchy vowels.

The Next Step

Now that you have progressed through the three primary vowels, the Practice Plans will have more variety. It is up to you how fast you will progress at this point in your study, so you will need to focus on the quality and consistency of the practicing to produce the best results.

Many singers want to know how long they should practice, and the answer varies with each individual. At a minimum, you need to practice fifteen to twenty minutes per day, five days a week. Your voice teacher or vocal coach can assist you in determining the right amount of time you should practice.

Corresponding Exercises, Practice Plans & Worksheets

Here are the exercises, Practice Plans, and worksheets for chapter 9:

The /ee/ Vowel

Practice Plan Descriptions

Worksheet 9

Available in the Member Download Library at VocalFitnessStudio.com

CHAPTER 10

RESPONSIVE BREATHING

The next step is to take the ideas of breathing to five and *breathe early, breathe often*, and integrate them into your practicing. The exercises in this chapter will guide and help you better understand the workings of the intercostal muscles, the feeling of compressed air in the lungs, and how to achieve the best active rib-cage posture.

Vocal Fitness Training's exercises seek to coordinate many separate muscle movements to teach you how to breathe for singing, as well as to make you aware of the mechanics of the respiratory muscles. You must not interfere with respiratory muscle movements to gain some sort of control over exhalation until you have developed fundamental breathing skills. For this reason, do not engage the abdominal muscles on your own yet. You are still in the learning stages, and you do not want to tighten up your breathing sequence inadvertently. When the exercises are done properly, the abdominal muscles will begin to reveal themselves so you can experience how the entire upper body participates in the breathing process.

PRACTICAL VOCAL SCIENCE

Before we explore how to develop breathing skills further, there is one important point you need to know: *the practicing of breath management must take place during the activity of singing*. Some people advocate practicing breathing exercises separately from singing, with the goal of strengthening the breath. One popular exercise, "shh shh shh shh shhhhhhh," certainly engages the breathing muscles, but it isolates breathing *without integrating phonation and articulation*.

Interestingly, the execution of strong articulation does tend to induce the body to take in more air to create vocal tone. This is not the only ingredient for successful breath management, but it does show us in a small way that the breath responds somewhat to the vocal requests we make. Unfortunately, that is not enough to improve your singing, and you still need to extend a helping hand by providing the proper amount of initial air and by maintaining enough air pressure to support a free vocal tone.

Well-designed vocal exercises will challenge the body and teach it how to respond to these actions of articulation. For example, if we artificially interrupt the phrase and put in an extra breath, the diaphragm will contract and the abdominal muscles will respond naturally to this request. Repeating this action sets up a pattern of breathing that helps to manage the breath in the context of singing.

Similar to what happens in the "shhh" exercise noted above, the singer will become aware of a bounce in the upper abdominal area, but the difference is that it occurs from vocalization and not as an intentional jerking or tightening of the abdominal muscles. In this way, the vocal exercise *teaches* the singer about breathing and begins the process of strengthening the muscles and increasing flexibility as a natural reflexive response to articulation.

Most singers want to learn how to control their exhalation, but we have to be careful not to make that the only focus of our breathing. There can be a detrimental effect of trying to control the exhalation on a long phrase by tightening your abdominals until your breath runs out. You might think (or have been taught) that this will eventually increase the ability to sing long phrases, but that kind of approach excludes the integration of the entire breathing mechanism.

Preparing for Vocal Exercises

Exploring the Lifted Rib Cage: Active Rib-Cage Posture

In chapter 8, you learned that creating a stream of pressurized air moves high-energy breath across the vocal cords, allowing them to vibrate easily. The next step is to develop a deeper understanding of pressurized breath and to begin to practice it in a manner that will maintain a strong flow of air.

Instruments such as the bagpipe or accordion have mechanical bellows that assist them with the use of pressurized or compressed air. For example, when the accordion player pulls their instrument apart, air is drawn into a chamber called the bellows. When the player pushes the bellows together, they force that compressed air over the internal reeds, producing sound. However, instead of closing the instrument completely, the player reverses direction at a point that maintains some air in the bellows. In this way, they leave a residual amount of air inside the instrument and avoid running out of air and tone.

You will use a similar process to send pressurized air across your vocal cords while maintaining a reasonable supply of residual air in your lungs. Constant muscle movement will strengthen the muscles that control the speed of the pressurized air for vocalization.

Remember Good Posture!

Posture is a critical component of breathing for singing, since correct body alignment balances all parts of the upper body. Therefore, the goal is to have your ribs comfortably lifted so they can be free to expand and work without great effort. It is much more difficult to breathe while even slightly slouching, because any collapsing of the upper body works against the breathing muscles, making it much harder work. Other things to remember include the following:

- Keep the abdominal muscles released as you inhale, and allow them to contract naturally on the exhalation.

- Make sure that you take the time to refill your lungs with a silent breath, as this encourages deep inspiration and helps to avoid falling into the trap of taking a shallow, gaspy breath.

- Sing these exercises at a moderate speed to allow you to regulate the flow of

- air naturally in and out of your lungs.

- Keep your breaths slow and silent. Avoid noisy breathing and gasping at all costs!

IN MY STUDIO

With so many new things to learn about vocal production, my students sometimes forget to focus on their breathing. I often have to remind them to breathe to five, and it amazes them at how big of a difference it makes to remember that one, simple step. Everyone knows that you need more air to sing, but most do not know how to manage the breath or realize how much consistent attention and practicing it takes to create new breathing habits.

I have had students who fall into a singing habit that I call the *singing-along syndrome*. This happens when the student sings along with music they enjoy without incorporating any vocal technique. They sing along while listening with either headphones or earbuds and often in a weak voice so as not to disturb others, all the while mimicking the singer's vocal style.

With so much amplification and audio editing done in the recording studio nowadays, many singers barely have to sing above speaking level to be heard. When my students copy that sound, they often do so using no more than the amount of air one would use to speak, which is obviously not enough to create a stand-alone singing tone. One can sing on a minimal amount of air, but the result is not going to enhance either your singing tone or your vocal health.

One way to begin integrating better breathing is to focus on it when you practice your vocal exercises. This will encourage the muscle memory you need to create new vocal habits.

THE NEXT STEP

By this time, you have learned a great deal about vocal production and breathing, and you have accumulated dozens of vocal exercises. To make things easier for you, the Practice Plans at the end of each chapter are cumulative of the materials presented up to that point, with the exercises organized in a specific order to work on specific areas of your voice over the course of five to seven days. Think of them as a ready-made sequence that takes the mystery out of what exercises you should practice from week to week.

CORRESPONDING EXERCISES, PRACTICE PLANS & WORKSHEETS

Here are the exercises, Practice Plans, and worksheets for chapter 10:

Responsive Breathing

Practice Plan Descriptions

Worksheet 8

Available in the Member Download Library at VocalFitnessStudio.com

CHAPTER 11
STRENGTHENING THE /EE/ VOWEL

This unit will explore the /ee/ vowel further with more challenging exercises to strengthen its production. You should be fluent in the proper positioning of the /ee/ vowel and setting of the hum before working through this next section.

If you feel you need to work a little longer on the /ee/ vowel, then discuss with your teacher about spending another week (or more) on one or more of the following: Practice Plan 11A, Practice Plan 11B, Practice Plan 12A, or Practice Plan 12B.

PRACTICAL VOCAL SCIENCE

The Role of Consonants as Tone Starters

Many different parts of the mouth, lips, and tongue produce consonant sounds, which help us determine the understanding of the basic components of syllables and words. When we speak, these sounds act as tone *stoppers*, as they delineate one word from another and turn what could otherwise be unintelligible sounds into comprehensible language.

However, since vowels are the primary carrier of tone when singing, the role of the consonant needs to change. Instead of being tone stoppers, they will propel the vowel sounds and act as tone *starters*. Since use of the consonants in this way assists in positioning the mouth properly to establish better acoustic resonance, effective vocal exercises done with strong consonant articulation from proper muscle positions encourages well-produced, healthy vocal sound.

Strengthening Articulation Using *k* and *h*

In previous exercises, we have used the consonant sound "y" to engage the tongue in the production of the open vowels /oo/ and /oh/. In chapter 9, we added humming with the consonant sound "m." We will continue to use those consonant and vowel combinations in vocal exercises, but, in order to strengthen the /ee/ vowel further and encourage an active interior articulation, we will use various articulations of the consonant *k*, followed by an extended articulation of the consonant *h*.

We will practice the *k* three ways: percussive ("kh"), with a short hiss ("khh"), and with an extended hiss ("khhhhh"). The number of *h* letters following the *k* will indicate the amount of hiss to produce. There certainly are other consonants that could help strengthen the /ee/ vowel, but the consonants *k* and *h* engage the back and sides of the tongue, and it is voiceless, encouraging vowel onset with a cushion

74

of compressed air. The important thing to remember is that due to its aspirant nature, this consonant avoids engaging the glottal stop at the voicing of the vowel.

All of these exercises are short in length, but you need to attain a degree of competency in each before moving ahead to the next one, so keep that in mind as you practice. These exercises will appear throughout your Practice Plans in the future, but you will not spend a lot of time practicing them after their introduction in this chapter. They are a means to an end, as they introduce you to a better understanding of what an active mouth feels like while at the same time strengthening the articulation of your tongue for the /ee/ vowel.

Voiceless Palatal Fricative!

Fun to say, *palatal fricative* is a term that aptly describes the production of certain consonants. Here is a brief description of the articulation positions within the mouth for a voiceless palatal fricative.

- *Voiceless* means that the vocal cords are not involved in pronouncing the consonant.

- *Palatal* refers to sounds created by the back half of the tongue contacting the hard palate.

- *Fricative* refers to the constriction of air as it flows through a narrow channel in the mouth. Another example of a fricative consonant is the letter *f*, where friction occurs in the small space between the top front teeth and the bottom lip.

In My Studio

One of the most common questions students ask me is if their singing (including performing) will include the overly exaggerated format found in these exercises. The answer is no, for the most part. The sole purpose of using exaggeration is to strengthen and condition the muscles used for singing.

For some students, exaggerated movement of the lips, cheeks, and facial muscles feels very awkward at first because they want to revert to their old habits. If they used to sing with a relaxed mouth, then their muscles will be understandably unfamiliar with the feeling of exaggerated movement.

Therefore, when you are practicing, observe yourself in a mirror to ensure that you are using the correct mouth position on each pronunciation. Keep in mind this important concept: *consistent repetition of the proper positions creates stronger muscle movements and, in time, better singing.* Once the muscles are stronger and more flexible, you will be able to release the exaggeration into a natural, but active, articulation.

THE NEXT STEP

Chapter 11 effectively ends the introduction of the three primary vowels /oo/, /oh/, and /ee/. At this point you have all of the basic tools you need to begin strengthening your voice and improving your singing. Please remember that your improvement depends upon deliberate practicing to train your muscles where to move and to develop the stamina they need to maintain a consistent vocal tone.

CORRESPONDING EXERCISES, PRACTICE PLANS & WORKSHEETS

Here are the exercises, Practice Plans, and worksheets for chapter 9:

Strengthening the /ee/ Vowel

Practice Plan Descriptions

Worksheet 11

Available in the Member Download Library at VocalFitnessStudio.com

CHAPTER 12
LEGATO AND VOCAL LINE

Smooth, connected tones are what you hear when listening to a well-trained or naturally gifted singer. This is referred to as vocal line, and it sounds like the voice is gliding along with a pleasant fluid quality to it. Although many singers have a flow to their singing, it is still important to learn strategies and techniques that give you skills to go beyond what you are already able to do.

PRACTICAL VOCAL SCIENCE

Using the Consonant *h*

Although the palatal fricative exercises are helpful for strengthening the tongue, singers also need to practice vowel exercises preceded by a slight sound of the consonant *h*. The use of the *h* to achieve articulation in singing is very common in both solo and choral settings. For example, many choir directors use it as a strategy to coordinate the efforts of a large group of people singing a series of notes all on one vowel. Teachers like this consonant because it keeps singers from beginning the vocal onset with a glottal stop.

Achieving Vocal Line

What most singers miss is the fact that in order for the air to sustain tone, you must stretch to form the positions to create the best possible acoustic resonance. If we need to create a successive string of sounds (singing one single vowel, for example), thinking of each vowel as a separate articulation will keep the sound moving from one pitch to the next.

Many singers make the mistake of starting to sing and then relaxing, thinking that their voice will keep going on its own. That will work to a certain extent, but once you have stopped stretching and pronouncing, the muscles will relax a bit and the vocal instrument will lose its line.

How Breathing Technique Enables Vocal Line

Vocal line imparts smoothness to your voice that makes it sound as if it will never end. The key to good line, or legato, is the ability of a singer to maintain a steady stream of air through the vocal tract without interruption. As we have learned, proper breath and a correctly formed vocal tract can help you accomplish this.

Think Your Way to Legato

We certainly can agree that your thoughts control the movement of your muscles. You think to yourself, "I am going to pick up that pencil," and you reach over and pick up the pencil. It is rather amazing, when you think of it (pun intended). Since muscle movement drives vocal production, it would follow that we can think our muscles into vocal actions. The only difference in singing is that you cannot see the results.

So, how do you think your way through your singing? Practice and focus. This may seem like a crazy idea at the outset, but it is strongly rooted in physiology. Without going into all of the scientific, neural, and anatomical movements, suffice to say that your brain controls your muscles, and your muscles will pretty much do what you think. That is the easy part to understand. *The hard part is practicing that approach.* You will learn about this in exercise 57, but it has a quirky instruction: You must simply engage your thoughts to sing!

In My Studio

Some of my students do not realize they will have to become familiar with phonetics when they embark on the journey of learning how to improve their singing. For most of us, we sing for the pure joy and fun of it, but, as the demands of our singing increase, we find that we hit a wall. That is often the point where we reach out for some type of vocal instruction to improve our singing production.

What also surprises many students is the realization that their voice is actually the sum of their vowel sounds. They have heard of vocal exercises, but they did not know about the emphasis on vowel formation. In the same way, most people do not know they should pay attention to consonants, or realize that the consonants' role in producing singing tone is somewhat different than in speech. When singers find out that they can actually think their way to better singing—well that is just the icing on the cake!

If you really think about it, it makes a lot of sense. Our speech is controlled by our thoughts, so why not our singing, too? The key is to do the hard work of training the muscles and their movement in an exaggerated way to strengthen their articulation and memory, so that when you do *think to sing*, the results will be appropriate for the demands placed upon them.

CORRESPONDING EXERCISES, PRACTICE PLANS & WORKSHEETS

Here are the exercises, Practice Plans, and worksheets for chapter 9:

Legato and Vocal Line

Practice Plan Descriptions

Worksheets 10 and 11

Available in the Member Download Library at VocalFitnessStudio.com

CHAPTER 13
STRETCHY VOWELS

This chapter will introduce you to a simple way to strengthen the articulation of other English vowel sounds. The goal is to practice vocal exercises on six additional common vowel sounds to create a consistent tone for each. Exaggerated articulation will continue to be the strategy used to make the muscles stronger and more flexible. Since vowel sounds carry most of the tone of singing, you need to spend practice time forming and creating common vowel sounds as the building blocks for your vocal tone. There is no substitute for practicing, and having a plan to improve your vowels is the smartest and most efficient way to achieve a better vocal tone. The vowels introduced so far have shown you the benefit of exaggerated articulation for creating acoustic resonance. The new vowel exercises are similar in design to previous patterns and give you a rich resource for training your instrument.

PRACTICAL VOCAL SCIENCE

Vowel sounds begin to develop in the vocal tract immediately above the vocal cords in the pharynx, and tongue and lip position will further modify or enhance them. The brain learns how to command this entire vocal-tract area into vowel positions when you're a baby, during speech acquisition. Ultimately, vowel sounds are created by thought: you think "ah" and your brain sends a message to your vocal tract, "Give me an *ah*," and the pharynx and the tongue respond with the position for "*ah*." As the sound waves travel upward through the pharynx and into the mouth cavity, it is the positions of the mouth, tongue, lips, and jaw that bestow the particular qualities that make it a vowel. In the end, a well-produced vowel equals a great tone, which is why all this fuss about vowels is so important.

The Concept of Vowel Sounds

Although the world's languages contain various vowel sounds, *Vocal Fitness Training* uses American English as the basis for its examples. To go into detail on other languages would be too time consuming here. If you sing in other languages, the principles and practices presented in this unit will still apply, and you may find that non-English languages (such as Italian) have fewer vowel sounds, and will be easier to navigate. Many good resources are available that cover both vocal diction for singers and standard phonetics.

Since American English draws much of its vocabulary from other languages, its words are often irregular in their pronunciation. Anyone familiar with English has surely encountered the challenges of these inconsistencies. As a result, there are differing opinions as to how many actual vowel sounds exist in English; depending on how someone counts them, there can be as many as twenty-nine or more!

As we continue the study of vowel sounds, be careful not to confuse them with the five vowel letters of the alphabet, *A, E, I, O,* and *U,* as each of them can represent many different sounds. The table below shows several examples of the different sounds made from the same letter.

Letter	A	E	I	O	U
Words	Path Face Hawk	Dress Fleece Eye	Kit Price	Boat Foot Goose Hot	Strut Cute Urge

It is clear from this chart that we will need to depend more on our ear than our sight to determine the vowel sound. It is important to know this because it will determine how you shape your mouth to create the best vowel tone.

Pronunciation Key

The ability to listen to and identify the vowel sounds is needed to improve your vowel production, and using representative symbols helps guide that identification. Most classical singers prefer using the International Phonetic Alphabet (IPA) symbol set. This is a product of the International Phonetic Association, which is the major representative organization for phonologists. The organization's aim is to promote the scientific study of phonetics and its applications. Its symbols are a widely accepted international notational standard for the phonetic representation of *all* languages. Although the IPA creates consistency and clarity, learning the system can be an unnecessary challenge. In order to keep things simple, the symbols appearing in this text are similar to those found in common grade-school texts.

On the next page is the phonetic symbol key for this book, which gives you a basic visual tool to represent the various vowel sounds.

Vowel Sound Symbols	As in...
ee	fleece, sea, beat, sweet
ā	face, hey, may, aid
ĭ	kit, bin, in, hymn
eh	dress, met, ten, said
ă	trap, map, back, can
ah	palm, bought, paw, all
ŏ	lot, song, off, clock
uh	strut, sung, ton, above
oh	goat, flow, sew, though
oo	goose, hue, through, new
ī	price, bright, life, height

You may notice in the chart above that there are symbols over some of the letters. These are diacritical marks, and the ones used here are the long vowel mark (¯) and the short vowel mark (˘). An easy way to remember the pronunciation of the long vowel sound is that you pronounce them exactly like the name of the letter, as you do while reciting the alphabet in American English. For example, the symbol for the letter A has a long vowel mark over it: **ā**.

GROUPING VOWEL SOUNDS ACCORDING TO MOUTH POSITION

Before we continue, it is important for you to understand that we will group vowels into simple mouth positions for the low to medium-high part of the vocal range. This is a short-term strategy to encourage strong, exaggerated articulation in the mouth. Once your muscles are stronger and more flexible and your mouth is more active, the external stretching will diminish significantly. Then, the vowels will fall into a more natural position as an internal stretch replaces the need for external exaggeration.

As you continue with your study of *Vocal Fitness Training*'s techniques, you will begin to realize that it is necessary to have constant internal stretching of the articulators during vocal production. Reducing the mouth positions of the remaining vowel sounds into two distinct groups is an intentional strategy, developed to reduce the amount of time spent in studying every single vowel-sound position. The bottom line is that we need to sing with strong, flexible muscles and to keep our tongue and the interior of our mouth active, and this is the quickest way to learn and strengthen the feeling of that internal stretch.

In previous units, we learned that /oo/ has a very strong forward postural position of the lips, and conversely, /ee/ has the opposite position with the mouth spread into a natural smiley stretch. The rest of the vowel sounds' positions lie somewhere in between these two opposing vowels. What's interesting is that we can use either of these two postural lip positions as a basis of articulation to strengthen the production and clarity of the vocal tone.

Using the Natural Smiley Stretch

You can enhance the vowels and make them easier to sing by using the natural smiley stretch on middle to low-range pitches. Stretching keeps the vowels connected so you will not relax and drop the articulation from syllable to syllable. This approach is extremely beneficial for beginning to intermediate singers, as its intention is to create both muscle strength and memory. Eventually you will be able to lift and stretch from the inside of the mouth, without the help of an external exaggerated position.

Vowels in the upper range incorporate a different mouth-positioning strategy, as the mouth needs a larger opening to eliminate vocal strain and to create a richer tone and a seamless melodic line. For the short term, most beginning students in this vocal technique need to strengthen their articulation, using the natural smiley stretch in the low and middle range only.

Another thing to keep in mind is that the natural smiley stretch needs to be in constant motion. Your stretch occurs through the full range of motion, as you pronounce each syllable. When you do this, it will help you to avoid the tendency to lock up your muscles.

Reduced Vowel Sounds' Mouth Positions

There are two vowel sounds that are not included in our chart or exercises. They are difficult to spot in the English language as they occur with numerous and different spellings. Both sounds exhibit a lack of stress or strength when pronounced and are referred to as *reduced* vowels. It is not necessary to give them a strong, exaggerated stretch, however some comment must be made about their mouth position in order to ensure that singers will produce them with an active articulation.

The schwa

ə

The schwa sound itself is somewhat neutral and often occurs in unstressed syllables such as the *o* in *reason*, the *ble* in *scribble*, and the *a* in *partial*, or the *ie* in *patience*, just to name a few. The schwa, although unstressed in speech, does require more articulation when singing, and, in general, the use of the natural smiley stretch will apply.

The horseshoe u

$$\bigcup$$

The horseshoe u sound occurs as the *u* in *put,* the *ou* in *should,* and the *oo* in *foot.* Like the schwa, it needs some attention when singing, so a slight pursing of the lips will help to keep its articulation active.

Vowel Exercises Using the Natural Smiley Stretch

Please do not expand the natural smiley stretch to the medium-high or upper range as the strategy presented here is specifically for the middle and low range. In addition, be sure to use the strong consonant indicated in each exercise to launch the physical stretching of the lips and cheeks, which will help to invoke the natural smiley stretch. Listen carefully to each track and copy the vowel sound as you hear it demonstrated.

Exaggeration Is a Tool

One concern that new students frequently have is that the exaggerated pronunciation will look ridiculous when they are performing. And to some degree, they are right! What you need to remember is that the exercises are just that, exercises. Just as the baseball player lifts weights so he can hit the ball farther but doesn't bring the weights to bat, once you reach the point of performing a song, your muscles will have begun to naturally stretch and produce the tones you desire. For the short term, though, exaggeration will be a useful tool as you improve your singing technique.

When to Release the Exaggerated Articulation

The goal of exaggerated articulation is to create new muscle movement and memory, as well as to exercise the muscles to develop flexibility and strength. Now that you have finished working through and learning all of the material in this book, you might be wondering when the exaggeration should end.

It varies with everyone, and it depends on whether or not the student's improvement means that there is no longer a need for the full exaggeration. This often becomes apparent when singing of a song, because constantly exaggerated movement from one syllable to another is difficult to maintain. Eventually, the exaggeration turns into a feeling of constant stretching, primarily inside your mouth. Remember, one of the goals is to create the correct acoustic-resonance space inside your mouth to encourage well-articulated vowels, which in turn produces a good vocal tone. There are two areas where you will change the exaggerated articulation in different ways.

Exercises

It is likely that you will not ever completely remove the exaggerated stretch from exercises. What will happen, though, is that your muscles will become more responsive, and it will become easier to execute the exercises. In the end, you may only decrease the exaggeration by 40 to 50 percent.

Songs

If you find that it is difficult to sing a song with the exaggerated mouth positions, try singing it with a step-down approach. There is not an exact way to determine how much to release, so first, try singing the song with a decrease of 10 to 15 percent stretch (using the mirror, of course) and see if you are still able to maintain an active mouth.

In order to determine if you are able to continue to produce a good vocal tone with this amount of release, you should either sing for another person or record yourself. If you are satisfied with the result, sing at that reduced exaggeration level for a while. After that, you can try releasing a little more exaggeration until you feel a strong but comfortable internal stretch from syllable to syllable. You will not eliminate the idea of exaggeration, but the stretch does become easier the more accomplished you are with the vocal technique.

In My Studio

Most of my students understand and apply the information in this chapter quickly, but the test seems to come when they have to figure out what vowel sounds are in a particular word. This is especially difficult for voice students still in school who are continuing to learn vocabulary and spelling.

It seems that the hardest vowel sound to recognize is the letter *o* in a word. The letter *o* by itself or in combination with other letters can represent many different vowel sounds. Then, there are other instances where the letters in a word are pronounced as the /oh/ sound, but there is no letter *o* indicated. Study these words and see just how varied spellings can be. Some contain the letter *o*, but sound like /oo/, and others have a letter *e* and sound like an /oh/! Here are several examples:

> oo — through
> oh — sew
> ah — cough
> oh — hoe
> uh — oven
> oh — dough

CORRESPONDING EXERCISES, PRACTICE PLANS & WORKSHEETS

Here are the exercises, Practice Plans, and worksheets for chapter 9:

Stretchy Vowels

Practice Plan Descriptions

Worksheet 12

Available in the Member Download Library at VocalFitnessStudio.com

Vocal Fitness Training Exercises and Practice Plans

Exercise 1

Spoken Separated /yoo/

Vocal Fitness Training's exercises include many spoken lessons because they are an effective way to prepare muscle pattern and habit. You should keep in mind that essentially the same physical mechanism produces both your speaking and singing voices. For that reason, as you continue with your vocal study and improve in your ability to use this technique, you should consider spending some time focusing on the improvement of your overall speaking voice.

This is particularly important for those of you who sing Contemporary Commercial Music (i.e., musical theater, pop, rock, folk, country, jazz, and blues), as those genres have firm roots in speech patterns. Also, if you have a habit of relaxing your articulation for speech regularly, it may be more challenging to access the greater muscle energy required for transforming those spoken sounds into strong and free singing tones. You will begin with spoken vocal exercises, since singing comes from speech and speaking in the midrange of your speaking voice lets you concentrate on form without the incurrence of pitch. You need to establish the proper form of the /oo/ exercises now in order to sing the counterpart of these exercises in later lessons.

1. Before you speak each exercise, breathe silently and slowly (one to three seconds) through your mouth. Incorporating this type of simple breathing begins to create new habits that encourage coordination of breath with phonation and vocalization.

2. Slowly speak the /yoo/ syllable five times in a row, separating each one with a stop.

3. Make sure you always practice with a mirror to check your form.

4. As you speak each syllable, make sure they are of equal duration.

5. Maintain the lips in a stretched position until after you stop the breath, in order to end the syllable cleanly. This may seem awkward at first, but it is an essential step to learn how to release the vocal sound properly.

6. As you speak this exercise, notice that the jaw naturally drops slightly to accommodate the /yoo/ sound. You may feel a small bit of space open up behind your upper and lower front teeth. If you do not feel that, you may need to enhance that space to create a more rounded tone. Rather than trying to manipulate the muscles, try imagining that there is a small grape sitting just behind your upper and lower front teeth. (Please note: do not actually put a grape there, as that would create a choking hazard!)

7. Repronounce every syllable with the same amount of energy as the first. Think of each note as a line segment (see below). This visual image will reinforce the physical positioning, resulting in a consistent vocal tone and encouraging the development of muscle strengthening and memory.

8. Repeat this sequence a minimum of three more times before going to the next exercise.

Audio Track and Video: 1S and 1V

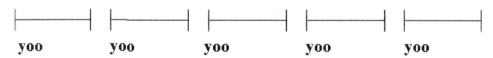

yoo　　　**yoo**　　　**yoo**　　　**yoo**　　　**yoo**

Exercise 2

Spoken Connected /oo-ee/

1. This vowel combination will exercise your facial muscles for strength and flexibility. Make sure to stretch through the entire range of motion of the muscles for each vowel sound as you did in Exercise 1.

2. Make sure you always practice with a mirror to check your form.

3. Before you speak each exercise, breathe silently and slowly (one to three seconds) through your mouth. Incorporating this type of simple breathing encourages you to begin to create new habits that encourage coordination of breath with phonation and vocalization.

4. Speak the /oo/ vowel with the forward stretch you learned in Exercise 1, followed by the /ee/ vowel.

5. Notice that when you pronounce the second syllable /ee/ your muscles move into a natural smiley stretch and the upper cheek muscles lift slightly.

Audio Track and Video: 2S and 2V

oo__ee oo___ee oo___ee oo___ee oo___

A slight "w" sound may occur as you change the /ee/, indicating that you are doing the exercise properly as you engage your lip muscles. If you are creating an /oo-wee/ sound, that is okay for now, as it indicates strong muscle engagement. Repeat steps 1-3 a minimum of three more times before going to the next exercise

Exercise 3

Spoken Connected /yoo/

The next step is to speak a series of connected /yoo/ syllables. As you connect the /yoo/ syllables together, you should notice that your lips move back slightly to initiate the pronunciation of the "y" consonant. Let that natural pronunciation of the "y" consonant sound draw your lips into a partial natural smiley stretch each time.

1. Before you speak each exercise, make sure to breath silently and slowly (one to three seconds) through your mouth. Incorporating this type of simple breathing encourages you to create new habits that will begin to coordinate phonation with vocalization.

2. Speak the /yoo/ syllable with the forward stretch you learned in Exercise 1.

3. As you speak each syllable, make sure they are of equal duration.

4. Connect each syllable together as you speak this sequence of five /yoo/ syllables in a row.

5. Repeat this sequence a minimum of three more times before going to the next exercise.

Audio Track and Video: 3S and 3V

yoo____yoo_____ yoo____yoo_____ yoo____

Hint: Some singers encounter difficulty with this syllable pattern because the result sounds and feels more like the /oo-ee/ combination of Exercise 2. If so, then try the following approach to improve the connection of the /yoo/ syllables:

Slowly speak two successive separated /yoo/ syllables (as in Exercise 1):

yoo____yoo____

1. Repeat the same sequence, but instead of stopping the sound after the first syllable, quickly pronounce the second syllable. If you are successful with this approach, you will see your lips pull back into a slight natural smiley stretch about halfway back to your cheeks.

yoo_____ yoo_____

2. When you are satisfied with the result of the previous step, continue by adding one syllable at a time, until you can successfully connect all five syllables in a row. Repeat this sequence a minimum of three more times before going to the next exercise. Here is the entire exercise:

yoo____yoo____
yoo____yoo____yoo____
yoo____yoo____ yoo____yoo____
yoo____yoo____yoo____yoo____yoo____

Exercise 4

Learn a Simple Song

Throughout this book, you will sing an arrangement of a verse from the song "How Can I Keep from Singing?" As you work through the book, sometimes you will sing the entire verse and other times you will use only a single line as an exercise. Below is the complete musical excerpt, but do not worry, as you do not need to know how to read music to learn the melody. Exercise 4 at the VocalFitnessStudio. com website is a sung version of the song so you can learn it by ear. Each of the four lines and their accompanying exercises will appear throughout the course, so it is important to take the time now to learn the entire song.

How Can I Keep From Singing?

Words by "Pauline T." 1868
Alternate Text by Jane Edgren

Robert Lowry, 1881
Arranged by Jane Edgren

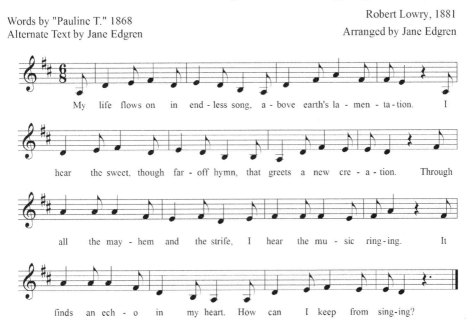

My life flows on in end-less song, a-bove earth's la-men-ta-tion. I

hear the sweet, though far-off hymn, that greets a new cre-a-tion. Through

all the may-hem and the strife, I hear the mu-sic ring-ing. It

finds an ech-o in my heart. How can I keep from sing-ing?

Exercise 5

Separated /yoo/

Sing /yoo/ five times in a row, separating each syllable with a stop (or breath), using the strong pronunciation you learned in Exercises 1–3.

In order to integrate the proper mouth movement fully, you will need to repeat each pitch example a minimum of three times.

1. In order to end the note cleanly, continue to stretch your lips until after you stop the breath. This may seem awkward at first, but it is an essential step to learn how to release the vocal sound properly.

2. You must repronounce every syllable within the scale with the same amount of energy as the first to develop a consistent muscle position. You will do this by restarting each syllable you sing using the exact mouth position as the previous one and by continuing the stretch throughout the duration of each pitch.

3. You should feel a slight pull on your cheek muscles as you pull your lips forward, and a small space about the size of a grape should open up behind your front teeth. You will feel and hear this from the inside as a muffled vibration in this part of your mouth. In the low range, your lips should be barely apart, with only a space about the size of a pencil eraser.

Audio Tracks and Video: 5D, 5A, and 5V

yoo   yoo   yoo   yoo   yoo

OTHER HELPFUL HINTS

Please note that as you work through improving these vowel sounds, the emphasis is on producing a stronger and more exaggerated position with the lips to encourage a better tone quality and to create muscle memory in the production of a particular vowel sound.

Exercise 6

Connected /oo-e/

You will sing a descending five-note scale in the same manner as in Exercise 2, but you will connect the syllables together, as you sing the double-vowel pattern /oo-ee/ on each note.

In order to integrate the proper mouth movement fully, you will need to repeat each pitch example a minimum of three times.

1. Sing the /oo/ vowel, with the forward stretch you used in previous exercises, followed by the /ee/ vowel.

2. Notice how the second syllable /ee/ moves your muscles into a natural smiley stretch with a slight lift of the cheek muscles.

3. You may notice a slight "w" sound when changing to the /ee/, which simply indicates that you are doing the exercise properly as you engage your lip muscles. If you are creating an "oo-wee" sound, that is okay for now, as it is a good indicator of strong muscle engagement.

Audio Tracks and Video: 6D and 6V

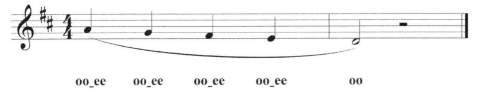

oo_ee   oo_ee   oo_ee   oo_ee   oo

Exercise 7

Connected /yoo-yoo/

The exercise consists of a descending five-note pattern on a connected /yoo-yoo/ similar to the one you learned in Exercise 3. As you sing each /yoo/, your lips will move back to initiate the pronunciation of the "y" consonant as in Exercise 3.

Remember to repeat each exercise a minimum of three times before moving to the next chord example.

Be careful not to lock your lips in a protruding fashion when you repeat the syllables. Instead, you need to repronounce each syllable as in previous exercises.

Audio Tracks and Video: 7D, 7A, 7L and 7V

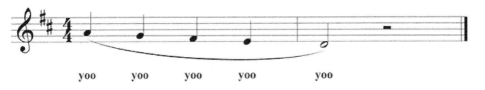

yoo   yoo   yoo   yoo   yoo

Hint: When you first begin this exercise, you may find that your result sounds and feels more like the /oo-ee/ articulation found in Exercise 6. If that is the case, it means that you are giving too much time to the pronunciation of the "y" consonant, and you need to sing the /oo/ vowel longer.

Practice the following sequence to improve the quick muscle change between the opposite positions of /oo/ and "y" and to facilitate pronouncing the vowel sooner:

1. Slowly sing two successive separated /yoo/ syllables (as in Exercise 1), to feel the exaggerated stretchy mouth position.

yoo_____   yoo_____

2. Sustain the first note of this two-note pattern for two or more beats, and, when you are ready, pronounce the second syllable quickly. You want to minimize the amount of time you pronounce the "y" consonant and move quickly to the / oo/ vowel. When done correctly, this should result in lip movement that pulls into a slight natural smiley stretch about halfway back to your cheeks as you start the second syllable.

3. Please note that these examples use half notes, but you do not have to sing them strictly for two beats. The dashed lines indicate that you are to sing the pitches as long as possible and to wait until you are ready to pronounce/sing the next syllable.

4. When you are satisfied with the result, continue by adding one syllable at a time until you can successfully connect all five syllables in a row with a strong /oo/ vowel predominant in the sound.

5. Return to the regular tempo of Exercise 7 and sing the connected /yoo-yoo/ patterns.

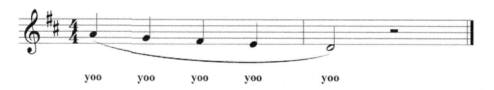

Exercise 8

Sustained Legato /yoo/

The next foundation exercise for /oo/ incorporates the same descending five note scale as previous tracks but removes the "y" consonant between the notes. This pattern is an example of sustained *legato* on a single vowel. Remember to repeat each exercise a minimum of three times before moving to the next chord example.

1. You should strengthen the articulation by protruding the lips in the /oo/ shape and stretching them forward continually through the phrase. This encourages the tongue to move into a natural stretched position, and keeps the tone steady throughout the exercise.

2. Maintain the exaggerated stretch of the lip muscles and cheeks for a moment after you release the breath.

Audio Tracks and Video: 8D, 8A, 8L and 8V

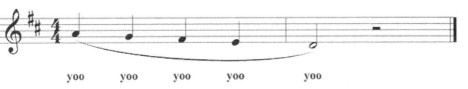

yoo   yoo   yoo   yoo   yoo

As you sing this scale, your lips should stretch forward while the opening between them narrows. My favorite image of this is looking through an old-fashioned spyglass from the wrong end, because the tube becomes narrower as you look through it from this perspective.

HELPFUL HINTS

The /oo/ vowel vocal exercise tone might sound somewhat hooty, even though you would not sing this vowel in a song with the same exaggeration. Nevertheless, if you hear this hooty, "covered," or "dark" tone, it is okay. Remember that the goal is to strengthen the muscle movements and positions resulting in the vocal exercise tone.

You have to remember that you are completely changing the way you make singing sounds. Moreover, just understanding the concepts intellectually does not mean that you will be consistent until you have developed new muscle memory.

As stated previously, the key to improvement is proper practicing. All of the tools you need to complete the exercises are in this book. You will improve if you practice, as long as you take your time to train your mind and muscles in the new movements.

THE PRACTICE ROOM

Practice Plan 1

Practice Plan 2

Practice Plan 3

Here are the essential guidelines for getting the most out of the Practice Plans:

- You can start any day of the week. To receive the most benefit from the Practice Plans, practice for six days before moving on. If you are following a shorter practice schedule (e.g., five days), simply practice the tracks on their indicated days.

- Practice daily, in the order listed, as the tracks are arranged in a specific sequence. Repeat each exercise a minimum of three times before moving to the next chord example. Think of this as the same as the reps you would do if you were lifting weights.

- Sing the exercises only as far in your range as is comfortable. Never force the sound, but allow your voice to improve naturally as you work it out over time.

- Practice all of the exercises in sequence on the given days, so you will get a variety of exercises that work out your voice and range.

- Always use a mirror to check your form and muscle movement.

- You are not limited to the exercises listed on any given day. You may add any other vocal exercise you have learned to your practice sessions.

- If you ever feel like you are having difficulty singing any of these exercises in the lower or higher part of your voice, such as experiencing tightening in the throat, stop immediately. The goal here is to exercise the muscles gently, and you have to give your body time to respond to the new tasks. Overworking the muscles to fatigue will be detrimental to your progress.

- The Practice Plan lists the exercise tracks in the order you will practice them. Remember to sing each example three times, in the same manner as you did in the lesson, checking your form in the mirror. Repeating the chord example multiple times is the same as the reps you would do if you were doing weight training at the gym. You need to create the muscle memory using the correct form to gain attain the desired results.

Exercise 9

Spoken Separated /yoo/ and /yoh/

1. Using a mirror, speak each syllable slowly and completely.

2. Keep the pronunciation strong throughout the duration of the vowel and release the sound by stopping the breath (avoid relaxing your lips to stop the sound).

3. Make sure that there is a complete silence between each syllable. As you speak this exercise, notice that the jaw drops slightly to accommodate the /yoh/ sound and a bit of space opens up behind your front teeth.

4. To enhance this stretch, imagine a marshmallow sitting just behind your upper and lower front teeth. (Please note: do not actually put a marshmallow there, as that would be a choking hazard!)

Audio Track and Video: 9S and 9V

/yoo/ /yoh/ - /yoo/ /yoh/ - /yoo/ yoh/ - /yoo/ /yoh/ - /yoo/

Exercise 10

Spoken Connected /yoo/ and /yoh/

As in the previous exercise, complete each syllable sound as you glide back and forth and notice how the cheek muscles become involved and assist with the heavy stretching. Encourage the use of these strong facial muscles, since they help to propel the lips into a strong forward position, maintain the position of the mouth, and cause the jaw to naturally open downward.

Audio Track and Video: 10S and 10V

yoo__yoh__yoo__yoh__yoo__yoh__yoo__ yoh__yoo__

Exercise 11

Sung Separated /yoh/

Similar to the strong articulation of the /yoo/ syllable, you will apply the same stretching position to the singing of the /yoh/ exercises by singing /yoh/ five times in a row, separating each one with a stop (or breath), and using the strong pronunciation described above. Remember to repeat each exercise a minimum of three times before moving to the next chord example.

1. Continue to stretch your lips until after you stop the breath to end the note cleanly. This may seem awkward at first, but it is an essential step to learn how to release the vocal sound properly.

2. You must repronounce every syllable within the scale with the same amount of energy as the first to develop a consistent muscle position. You will do this by restarting each syllable you sing using the exact mouth position as the previous one and by continuing the stretch throughout the duration of each pitch.

3. You should feel a slight pull on your cheek muscles as you pull your lips forward, and a bit of space should open up behind your front teeth that should feel larger than the /yoo/ syllable. You will feel and hear this from the inside as a muffled vibration in this part of your mouth.

Audio Tracks and Video: 11D, 11A, and 11V

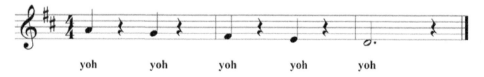

yoh   yoh   yoh   yoh   yoh

Exercise 12

Spoken Separated /yoh-yā/

The goal is to stretch and flex the facial muscles to strengthen these two positions for vowel production. The alternating vowel will be /ā/ (as in the word face) with a slight natural smiley stretch on that vowel. Remember to repeat each exercise a minimum of three times before moving to the next chord.

Audio Track and Video: 12S and 12V

/yoh-yā/ /yoh-yā/ /yoh-yā/ /yoh-yā/ /yoh/

Exercise 13

Spoken Connected /oh-ā/

As in Exercise 2, the goal is to create a smooth glide between the two vowels. You may note a slight "w" sound when changing to the /ā/, which is fine, since it will assist you in strengthening the muscles. Remember to repeat each exercise a minimum of three times before moving to the next chord.

Audio Track and Video: 13S and 13V

oh__ā__oh__ā__oh__ā__oh__ā__oh__

Exercise 14

Sung Connected /oh-ā/

Remember to repeat each exercise a minimum of three times before moving to the next chord example.

1. Sing the five-note scale below, alternating between /oh/ and /ā/ and connecting the syllables together.

2. Stretch the facial muscles into a slight natural smiley stretch, much the same as you did with the /oo-ee/ vowel combination in Exercise 6.

3. You may notice a slight "w" sound when switching between the /oh/ and the /ā/, which indicates that you are doing the exercise properly as you engage your lip muscles.

Audio Tracks and Video: 14D, 14A, and 14V

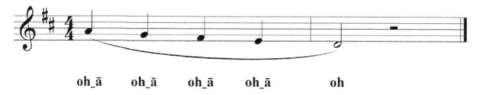

oh_ā   oh_ā   oh_ā   oh_ā   oh

Exercise 15

Simple Breathing Exercise

This initial breathing exercise introduces you to two strategies to help get you started with better breathing for singing, using an excerpt from the song "How Can I Keep from Singing?" You can sing this exercise by looking at either the music or the lyrics.

Breathe early, breathe often. In both examples, you will notice very large apostrophes inserted in the text every few words. This symbol is a breath mark, and it indicates where you take a breath. The placement of these particular breath marks encourages the breathe early, breathe often strategy. At first, you should not sing this exercise in tempo. Take time to breathe so that you are creating both muscle flexibility and memory. Remember to breathe slowly and silently before singing each group of words. You want to avoid taking gaspy breaths, at all costs.

Audio Track 15: "How Can I Keep from Singing?"

My   life flows on   in   end-less song,   a - bove earth's   la - men - ta - tion.

LYRICS

My life flows on,' in endless song,'

above earth's,' lamentation.'

100

Exercise 16

Spoken Separated /whoo/ /whoh/

Exercise 16 is similar to Exercise 14, as you will remove the initial pronunciation of the "y" consonant. The challenge here is to speak these vowels without a glottal initiation and to encourage a healthy vocal onset with air instead.

One way to do that is to start each vowel with a "wh" consonant sound, as in the word whoo. The "wh" consonant is voiceless, allowing the tone to originate completely from the airstream. This helps to train you to initiate sound on the breath and eliminates the tendency to grip these vowels with the laryngeal muscles as often happens with a glottal onset.

The "wh" consonant also engages the lip muscles and helps create a strong acoustic resonating chamber within the front of the mouth. Eventually you will drop the "wh" sound in favor of a balanced onset provided by a coordination of breath and vocal-cord position.

Remember to repeat each exercise a minimum of three times before moving to the next chord example.

Audio Track: 16S

/whoo_whoh/ /whoo_whoh/ /whoo_whoh/ /whoo_whoh/ /whoo/

Exercise 17

Spoken Connected /oo-oh/

This next exercise removes the "wh" consonant sound and connects the sounds together. Notice the position of your mouth as the lips form a partial "w" shape when you alternate between the two vowels. Speak this combination slowly, engaging the stretch of your mouth, lips, and tongue. Remember to repeat each exercise a minimum of three times before moving to the next example.

Audio Track: 17S

oo__oh__ oo__oh__ oo__oh__ oo__oh__oo__

Exercise 18

Sung Connected /yoh-yoh/

This exercise consists of a series of connected /yoh/ syllables. As you sing each one, your lips will move back each time to initiate the pronunciation of the "y" consonant similar to the /yoo/ in Exercise 7.

Remember to repeat each exercise a minimum of three times before moving to the next chord example.

1. Sing a descending five-note pattern similar to the /yoo/ in Exercise 7.

2. Be careful not to lock your lips in a protruding fashion.

3. Repronounce each syllable as in previous exercises.

4. There will be slight recoil to a natural smiley stretch at the beginning of each syllable as you pronounce the "y" consonant.

Audio Tracks: 18D, 18A, and 18L

yoh   yoh   yoh   yoh   yoh

Exercise 19

Sustained Legato /yoh/

Our next foundation exercise for /oh/ incorporates the same legato five-note scale as in previous exercises, but removes the "y" consonant between the notes. Sing the following five-note scale as a sustained legato on the /oh/ vowel.

You should strengthen the articulation by protruding the lips in the /oh/ shape and stretching them forward continually through the phrase. This encourages the tongue to move into to a natural stretched position, and keeps the tone steady throughout the exercise, similar to Exercise 7. Remember to repeat each exercise a minimum of three times before moving to the next chord example.

1. Be careful not to drop off your energy and/or relax the pronunciation on the last two notes of this descending scale, as it requires constant energy to produce the sound.

102

2. Maintain the exaggerated stretch of the lip muscles and cheeks for a moment after you release the breath.

Audio Tracks: 19D and 19A

yoh

THE PRACTICE ROOM

- Start any day of the week.

- Practice daily, in the order listed.

- Repeat each exercise a minimum of three times before moving to the next

- chord example.

- Sing the exercises only as far in your range as is comfortable. Never force the sound, but allow your voice to improve naturally.

- Avoid pushing out the tone or singing too loudly in an attempt to counter-intuitive your voice. Instead, start out by singing the exercise at half volume (or lower) while maintaining the exaggerated stretch. Although this may seem counterintuitive, it will allow the muscles to find new positioning, resulting in better vocal production overall. Once they are stronger, the acoustic reso-nance created by the new internal positions will set up a more productive way to increase the volume.

- Always use a mirror to check your form and muscle

Practice Plan 4

This Practice Plan includes the spoken /yoo/ and /yoh/ and the sung separated /yoh/ from exercises 9-11.

Practice Plan 5A

Practice Plan 5B

These Practice Plans add the vowel combination /oh-ay/ and the breathe early, breathe often concept introduced in exercises 12-15.

- You may notice a slight "w" sound when switching between the /oh/ and the /ā/, which indicates that you are doing the exercise properly as you engage your lip muscles.

- In order to create good vocal tone, and to keep your voice healthy, you must learn to breathe early and breathe often. Using this method refills the lungs so that you can benefit from singing on a cushion of residual air.

Practice Plan 6A

Practice Plan 6B

These Practice Plans contain the concept of the "wh" consonant, the vowel combination /oo-oh/, connected /yoh-yoh/, and the sustained legato on /yoh/ as presented in exercises 16-19.

- Remember, the "wh" consonant engages the lip muscles and helps create a strong acoustic resonating chamber within the front of the mouth. Eventually you will drop the "wh" sound in favor of a balanced onset provided by a coordination of breath and vocal cord position.

- There will be slight recoil to a natural smiley stretch at the beginning of each syllable as you pronounce the "y" consonant in the connected /yoh-yoh/ exercise.

- Be careful not to drop off your energy and/or relax the pronunciation on the last two notes of the sustained legato /yoh/ scale. Also, maintain the exaggerated stretch of the lip muscles and cheeks for a moment after you release the breath.

<u>Exercise 20</u>

Bent Cries on /yoo/

You will begin with two bent cries to initiate a proper stretch inside your mouth followed by a cry that spans an interval of a fifth. To sing the bent cry, you will sing the initial pitch and then end it as if you were speaking. Although the exercise pattern only indicates the singing of two bent cries, when you are learning this initially, you may need to sing several more before attempting the third cry.

The idea is to train your muscles in this new movement so that the third cry will be initiated in the same way as the bent cries. When you do sing the third cry, move quickly across the interval of the fifth. This allows the muscles to learn to navigate the movement without trying to control the speed of a slower cry.

Be careful, though, that you do not skip to the bottom note of the cry. If you find that you are skipping, take a few moments and do some sirens up and down the range of your voice to help you find that type of vocalization. As mentioned before, you may need to tap into some silliness here and imitate the sound of a fire truck! Additionally, you can sing the first note of the fifth cry for two beats before starting the cry to give yourself a little time to prepare mentally.

Also, if you are stretching your lips correctly, you may experience a slight "wh" sound as you release the /oo/. Although not ultimately desirable, this release is fine while you are learning the cries. As you become more accomplished, the "wh" sound will disappear, replaced by a strong lip stretch.

You do not have to do this exercise in tempo (strict time) when you are first learning this exercise. In fact, it is vitally important that you do this pattern slowly and methodically so that you create the correct muscle memory for the initiation of the cry. The tempo will come after you have mastered the pattern.

Remember, in order to integrate the muscle movement fully on a specific pitch set, you will need to repeat the entire example at least three times. Make sure you are observing and adjusting your mouth movements with a mirror.

Audio Tracks and Video: 20D, 20A, and 20V

Exercise 21

Cries in Fifths on /yoo/

This exercise is a variation of Exercise 20 but excludes the bent cry portion. Although similar, the goal for this exercise is to be able to start the cry immediately and sing the glide bit longer over the interval of the fifth. Do not worry if you are unable to accomplish this right away. It may take some time to get the coordination of the fifth cries, but they will improve with deliberate practicing and eventually will become a part of your standard repertoire of vocal exercises. Here are some things to remember:

- It is vitally important to avoid holding your breath as you initiate the cries.

- Similar to the legato you sang in Exercise 8, you will narrow your mouth as

- you glide through the interval of five pitches (think of a spyglass).

- When you reach the last pitch, sing it completely, release it properly, and continue stretching your lips until after you release the breath.

- Remember, in order to integrate the muscle movement fully on a specific pitch set, you will need to repeat the entire example a minimum of three times.

- Make sure you are observing and adjusting your mouth movements with a mirror.

Audio Tracks and Video: 21D, 21A, 21L, and 21V

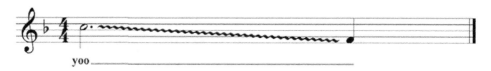

Exercise 22

Cry and Legato Scale on /yoo/

The following exercise encourages the stretch of the cry when singing a legato scale. Start by singing the cry and then repeat the same articulation with your lips and mouth as you move from pitch to pitch singing the descending scale. This exercise shows you for the first time how the cry can become the basic vocal sound for singing all pitches.

Audio Tracks and Video: 22D, 22A, and 22V

The Practice Room

The following Practice Plans are a bit longer, and are approximately eighteen to twenty minutes in length.

Practice Plan 7A

Practice Plan 7B

These Practice Plans contain the vocal cry exercises as presented in exercises 20-22. Here are some things to remember:

- It is vitally important to avoid holding your breath as you initiate the cries.

- Make sure you are observing and adjusting your mouth movements with a mirror.

- When you reach the last pitch, sing it completely, release it properly, and continue stretching your lips until after you release the breath.

Other Helpful Hints

Breath is probably the single most important coordinating activity for developing a strong cry in the voice. Make sure that you breathe silently and slowly, and when you are comfortably full of air, allow the breath to spill into the cry. Be very careful not to hold your breath before the vocalization, but allow the flow of the air to initiate the vocal sound and carry it through the exercise.

Make sure that you are producing an even siren quality. Some may have trouble at first with the final notes skipping a bit. If that is the case, go back to a faster execution of the fifth cry. If it continues to elude, make a sound like a fire truck siren to experience the natural progression of pitches. Then return to the cry exercises and fit that into the cry vocalization.

The speed of the cry is not as important as the singing of the glissando evenly. The vocal cords and laryngeal muscles will move the same amount regardless of the speed. As you improve, you will be able to slow down the cry to gain more benefit from the exercise.

Exercise 23

Rag Doll Roll Up

The ideal posture for singing is one that aligns the body naturally, allows for the free movement of the ribs and lungs, and balances the body without tension. It is surprising how quickly a change in posture will significantly change the vocal production. There are a number of ways to find good posture for singing, but a simple body roll-up exercise, when done correctly, frees the upper body, shifts the center of gravity to the lower body, and gives the singer a new paradigm of balanced posture.

Video: 23V

1. Place your feet shoulder distance apart, toes pointing forward. Slightly bend your knees and relax your upper body.

2. Release your upper body and lean over as far as you comfortably can (the object is to roll up, not see if you can touch your toes!). Make sure you release your neck and that your head and arms are free and dangling downward.

3. As you slowly begin to roll up, put the image in your mind of stacking your vertebrae one at a time.

4. Roll up at a moderately slow speed, but not a crawl. Your hips should remain constant, and resist the urge to rock them forward as you come up. (You may want to breathe in on the way up, but not while you are learning the basics. Focus first on form and movement, and add the breath once you have learned the exercise well.)

5. When you are all the way up, slowly float up your head until your chin is parallel with the floor. Be careful not to lift your chin too high or come up too fast. If you have long hair, do not to shake it out of the way, because that will upset the alignment of the neck and negate the whole point of the exercise. You may clear it out of the way with your hands when you are finished.

6. Next, slowly lift your shoulders straight up toward your ears, in a shrug.

7. Gently, and slowly move the shoulders slightly back, horizontal to the floor. You may feel your shoulder blades move together, but do not force that movement.

8. Release the shoulders gently, allowing them to settle into place (you may notice a slight shift forward and down as they return to their natural position).

9. Take one foot and move it slightly behind the other, shifting your weight to that foot. You do not need to sing with your weight equally balanced on both feet, but you should stand comfortably with the weight on one foot or the other, as you normally would.

When done correctly, the roll-up exercise will change your posture, assisting with your breathing and overall performance presentation. It is important to remember that this posture is not just for singing, so you must begin to incorporate this balanced posture into your everyday life.

Some of you may be familiar with this roll-up movement from yoga. It is essentially the same, but please note that the addition of steps 6, 7, and 8 help to align the shoulders. With all of our computer and smartphone use these days, as well as over-loaded backpacks, there is a tendency for many people to hunch their shoulders forward, moving the body out of alignment. Taking a moment to balance your shoulders goes a long way toward improving posture. You can do the shoulder adjustment steps outside of the Rag Doll Roll Up throughout the day if you feel you need to work on your shoulder position.

Exercise 24

Determining the Inspiratory Capacity, or Breathing to Six

1. Find your correct posture, breathe easily, and relax your abdominal area.

2. Breathe silently and slowly through your mouth until you have filled up your lungs completely with air. As you do this, notice the lateral expansion of the ribs on the sides of your body and feel how they lift upward near the end of the breath. When you are completely full of air, your shoulders may also rise up considerably (which is okay for this exercise).

3. Hold the breath for one second and then release all of the air at once. We call this full capacity position six (remember these numbers refer to average maximum amounts of air capacities). Do not hold your breath for more than a second, to avoid becoming lightheaded.

4. It is extremely important to rest for a few minutes before repeating this exercise, to avoid hyperventilating.

The intercostal muscles, which move your ribs, cause the movement you feel on the sides of your upper body. To explore the sensation of rib expansion and intercostal muscle movement further, repeat this activity one or two more times, with adequate rest in between to avoid dizziness.

Exercise 25

Measuring Rib-Cage Expansion to Determine the Inhalation Values

The following exercise will acquaint you with the significant physical expansion of your rib cage and show you how to understand the workings of the intercostal muscles as they relate to inhalation.

This exercise shows you how to become aware of the movement of the rib cage as the lungs fill with air. You will use a simple measuring tape and track the changes in your rib-cage expansion as you breathe. Then you will use those numbers to help determine the approximate capacity positions. The first inhalation position you will find is four, which is about halfway between resting position (two) and the full capacity position (six). From that data, you will be able to locate your approximate position five.

Find your correct posture, breathe easily, and relax your abdominal area. Do not, under any circumstances, tighten your stomach or abdominal area.

Place a measuring tape around your chest at the level of your front bottom ribs and breathe normally. Take two measurements: one as you breathe in and one as you breathe out. Add these numbers together and divide by two to get your average resting measurement. If you do not have a measuring tape, you can use a string, scarf, or anything that you can easily wrap around your rib cage and measure.

Breathe through your nose and inhale slowly while allowing your ribs to lift and expand all the way to six. Hold your breath for a moment while you take a measurement around your rib cage, and then exhale.

Inhale again slowly but stop when you reach the midpoint between the measurements taken in steps 2 (resting) and 3 (completely full). This is will give you the approximate measurement of position four or the midpoint in your breath. For example, if you have an average resting measurement of 34 inches and your maximum expansion measurement is 36 inches, then position four would be at approximately 35 inches.

To determine position five, calculate the distance halfway between positions four and six. In this example, that would be at approximately 35.5 inches.

Please understand that this is not an exact position of five, but a way to help you to begin to locate the comfortably full position. You might need to breathe a little more or a little less, that will become apparent the more you practice this type of inhalation. Also, keep in mind that as you improve your inhalation volume, the muscles will become more accustomed to this movement and gain more flexibility and strength. Therefore, this number could change as you improve the ability to increase the amount of air you inhale.

Possible Sample Measurements		
Sensation	Measurement in Inches	Approximate Capacity Number
Lungs Completely Filled	36	6
Position Five	35.5	5
Inhalation Midpoint	35	4
Resting Position	34	2

Another Way to Find Position Five

Another way to find position five involves a bit more awareness of the intercostal muscles and ribs, as well as someone to give you feedback on the expansion of the rib cage. Have someone you trust stand behind you and place their hands flat on each side of your rib cage, with each pinky finger resting just below the bottom rib. They should have their hands firmly on your ribs, pressing just enough for you to be able to feel your rib cage move against them.

1. Breathe to position six, to give both of you a sense of how the feedback works.

2. Next, breathe until your helper feels a slight upward change in direction of the ribs near their pinkie finger. As you initially breathe in, the ribs generally will expand sideways, but as you approach position five, both of you will feel additional expansion around the bottom edge of the rib cage. The point at which you feel this change in direction is approximately position five.

You could try this activity without a helper, using the back of one hand pressing against your ribs, because trying to place both hands (palm side down) on your rib cage will disturb your posture. Some students are able to get some feedback with this approach.

Even though both breathing activities can help you find an approximate position to breathe into, the goal is really about learning how to identify your comfortably full feeling, or position five. Keep in mind that once you determine the measurements for position five, or find that kick-out of the rib cage, you still may have to adjust your perception by inhaling either a little more or less air until you discover what comfortably full feels like.

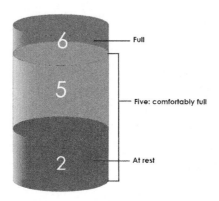

Exercise 26

Coordinating Phonation with the Breath

Breathing exercises done without singing can strengthen muscles, but they can miss the mark because they do not coordinate the breath with the onset of vocal sound. It is important to remember that when you practice, you need to integrate the breathing with the activity of singing in order to synchronize the entire process. The following exercise will invoke the coordination of the breath with phonation (singing).

1. Find the correct posture.

2. Breathe silently through your mouth and observe the expansion of the ribs caused by the movement of the intercostal muscles until you are at position five (comfortably full).

3. As soon as you reach position five, sing a single note of any pitch on the syllable /yoo/ for a count of three. Be careful not to hold your breath before you sing!

112

4. As you sing the note, maintain and stretch through the lip positions for / oo/. Release the note by stopping the breath, while keeping the lips in the stretched position. Do not stop the note by relaxing your mouth or lips.

5. After the note stops, you may relax your lips.

Exercise 27

Half Note Breathing on /yoo/

The next exercise reinforces the concept of taking a breath before you actually run out of air, but it utilizes your new knowledge of position five. Remember, the idea is to keep a reservoir of air in your lungs to act as a platform from which you will breathe. If you sing to the end of your breath, you will eliminate this extremely valuable resource.

Please sing this exercise slowly, with careful emphasis on taking in an initial slow, silent breath to position five. From this point forward, the phrase breathe to five will replace the former instruction breathe to position five (or the comfortably full position). Some things to remember:

- Breathe to five at the beginning of the exercise.

- Sing each note of the scale for two beats.

- During the rest, breathe back to five. Make sure that you do not release the breath in the rest but refill silently.

- Release each note by stopping the breath while keeping the lips in the stretched position. Once the note stops, then you may relax your lips and exhale.

- Do not stop the note by relaxing your mouth.

Remember to repeat each exercise a minimum of three times before moving to the next chord example.

Audio Tracks: 27D and 27A

yoo_____ yoo_____ yoo_____ yoo_____ yoo_____

113

The Practice Room

Practice Plans 8 and 8B

Each day will begin with Exercise 7D to warm up your voice. Do not skip this exercise as it is an integral part of each day's Practice Plan. This will increase your practice session by approximately two minutes.

Make sure that the following activities occur during this week's Practice Plan:

- Do a Rag Doll Roll Up (Exercise 23) to establish your posture before each track.

- Breathe to five before you sing each exercise example.

Exercise 28

Bent Cries on /yoh/

Similar to Exercise 20, you will begin with two bent cries to initiate a proper stretch inside your mouth, followed by a cry that spans an interval of a fifth. To sing the bent cry, you will sing the initial pitch and then end it as if you were speaking. Although the exercise pattern only indicates the production of two bent cries, when you are learning this initially you may need to sing several more before attempting the third cry. The idea is to train your muscles in this new movement so that the third cry will integrate that form.

When you do sing the third cry, move quickly across the interval of the fifth. This allows the muscles to learn to navigate the movement without trying to control the speed of the cry.

Be careful, though, that you do not skip to the bottom note of the cry. If you find that you are skipping, take a few moments and do some sirens up and down the range of your voice to help you find that type of vocalization. As mentioned before, you may need to tap into some silliness here and imitate the sound of a fire truck! Additionally, you can sing the first note of the fifth cry for two beats before starting the cry to give yourself a little time to prepare mentally.

Also, if you are stretching your lips correctly, you may experience a slight "wuh" sound as you release the /oh/. Although not ultimately desirable, this release is fine while you are learning the cries. As you become more accomplished, the "wuh" sound will disappear and be replaced by a strong lip stretch.

You do not have to do this exercise in tempo (strict time) when you are first learning the breath and voice coordination. In fact, it is vitally important that you do this pat-

114

ern slowly and methodically so that you create muscle memory for the coordination of the breath and vocal onset of the cry. The tempo will come after you have mastered the pattern. This is a great exercise for voice building, so you want to be sure you learn how to execute it properly while incorporating the breath.

Remember, bent cries initiate a proper stretch inside your mouth. You will sing the initial pitch and then bend it a bit, ending it as if you were speaking. Breathing to five and singing cries are part of a strategy to strengthen the coordination of your voice and breath. To do this effectively, follow the instructions below:

1. Breathe to five.

2. As soon as you have the proper amount of air, sing one bent cry. It is important to do this a few times before proceeding, in order to ascertain the coordination of the inhalation with the onset of the cry note.

3. Remember to sing the third cry over an interval of a fifth quickly. This allows the muscles to learn to navigate the movement without trying to control the speed of the cry.

4. Make sure that you give yourself enough time to breathe back to five before singing each syllable.

Remember to sing the last cry in the pattern quickly, and to repeat each exercise a minimum of three times before moving to the next chord example.

Audio Tracks: 28D and 28A

yoh _____   yoh _____   yoh _____

Exercise 29

Cries in Fifths on /yoh/

This exercise is a variation of Exercise 28, but it excludes the bent cry. The goal for this exercise is to be able to start the cry immediately and sing the glide bit longer over the interval of the fifth. Do not worry if you are unable to accomplish this right away. It may take some time to get the coordination of the fifth cries with the breathing, but they will improve with deliberate practicing, and eventually this will become a part of your standard repertoire of vocal exercises.

Here are some things to remember:

- It is extremely important to properly breathe to five before you sing the cries and to avoid holding your breath.

- Similar to the legato you sang in Exercise 8, you will narrow your mouth as you glide through the interval of five pitches (think of a spyglass).

- When you reach the last pitch, sing it completely, release it properly, and continue stretching your lips until after you release the breath.

- Remember, in order to integrate the muscle movement fully on a specific pitch set, you will need to repeat the entire example a minimum of three times.

- Make sure you are observing and adjusting your mouth movements with a mirror.

Remember to repeat each exercise a minimum of three times before moving to the next chord example.

Audio Tracks and Video: 29D, 29A, 29L, and 29V

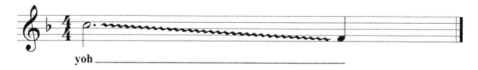

yoh

Exercise 30

Cry and Legato Scale on /yoh/

This next exercise encourages the stretch of the cry when singing a legato scale. Start by singing the cry and then repeat the same articulation with your lips and mouth as you move from pitch to pitch singing the descending scale. Always breathe to five before starting the exercise.

Remember to repeat each exercise a minimum of three times before moving to the next chord example.

Audio Tracks: 30D and 30A

THE PRACTICE ROOM

Practice Plans 9 and 9B

Each day will begin each day with Exercise 7D to warm up your voice. Do not skip this exercise as it is an integral part of each day's Practice Plan. This will increase your practice session by approximately two minutes.

Make sure that the following activities occur during this week's Practice Plan:

- Do a Rag Doll Roll Up.

- Breathe to five before you sing each exercise example.

Exercise 31

Half Note Breathing on /yoh/

You will begin with an exercise similar to Exercise 27, to prepare your breathing. Remember, the idea is to take a breath before you actually run out of air, keeping a reservoir of air in your lungs. If you sing to the end of your breath, you will eliminate this extremely valuable resource. Please sing this exercise slowly, with careful emphasis on taking in an initial slow, silent breath to position five.

Some things to remember:

1. Breathe to five at the beginning of the exercise.

2. Sing each note of the scale for two beats.

3. During the rest, breathe back to five. Make sure that you do not release the breath in the rest but refill silently.

4. Release each note by stopping the breath while keeping the lips in the stretched position. Once the note stops, then you may relax your lips and exhale.

5. Do not stop the note by relaxing your mouth.

yoh_____ yoh_____ yoh_____ yoh_____ yoh_____

Exercise 32

Breathe after Three on /yoo/ and /yoh/

The intention of these exercises is to make you breathe early after only singing three notes. This interrupting-breath exercise will begin to teach you how it feels to naturally refill the lungs while maintaining a cushion of air within them. As you become more competent, you will be able to sing in tempo and the breathing will become quicker. Remember to repeat each exercise a minimum of three times before moving to the next chord example.

1. Breathe to five.

2. Breathe after the third note each time. It is okay to interrupt the tempo of this exercise to refill the lungs. Take time to breathe fully to five after the third note.

3. Important! Do not hold your breath before singing!

4. Allow the air to flow into your body when you take the second breath. There is no trick to this; simply breathe to five again. Take your time!

Audio Tracks and Video: 32D, 32A, and 32V

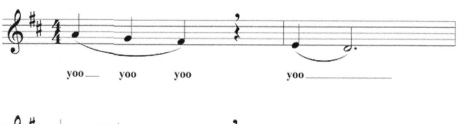

yoo___ yoo yoo   yoo___

yoh yoh yoh   yoh yoo

Exercise 33

Breathe Before You Need To / Breathe Early, Breathe Often

Another piece of this initial training is to return to the song "How Can I Keep from Singing?" and expand the breathe early, breathe often strategy you practiced in Exercise 4 to include the entire song. The goal is to honor the breath marks and begin to integrate the breathing cycle into a short musical phrase.

How Can I Keep From Singing?

Words by "Pauline T." 1868
Alternate Text, Jane Edgren

Robert Lowry, 1881
Arranged by Jane Edgren

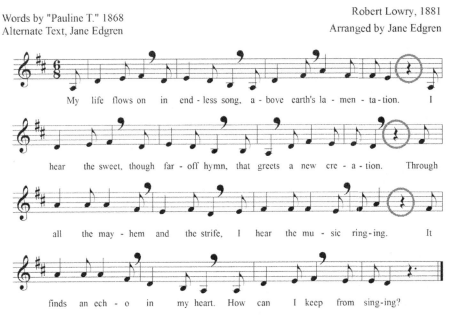

1. First, you will sing this selection by stopping at each breath mark and slowly breathing back to five. This readies your body for the muscle movement need-ed to refill your lungs quickly in tempo. Allow the air to flow into your body at the breath marks. There is no trick to this; simply breathe to five again. Take your time!

2. After you have sung through the selection several times, you will take silent breaths in tempo at the breath marks and then stop at the end of the line and breathe to five at the circle. Be careful not to release the air when you re-breathe. Do this several times until you start to feel the coordination of the tempo and the breath.

3. Important! Do not hold your breath at any time before singing!

4. Remember to breathe silently at the breath marks. You want to avoid taking gaspy breaths, at all costs.

HOW CAN I KEEP FROM SINGING?
**My life flows on' in endless song,'
above earth's' lamentation.**

(breathe to five)
**I hear the sweet' though far-off hymn,'
that greets' a new creation.**
(breathe to five)
**Through all the mayhem' and the strife,'
I hear the music' ringing.**
(breathe to five)
**It finds an echo' in my heart.'
How can I keep' from singing?**

Exercise 34

Singing Longer Phrases with Fewer Breaths

Sing the song with fewer breaths, and notice how the breath aligns with the lyrics in a more natural manner. The breaths indicated in this exercise are more like those you would normally take.

Similar to Exercise 33, stop at each breath mark and slowly breathe back to five. After you have sung through the selection several times, you will take in silent breaths in tempo at the breath marks but stop at the red circle and take a full breath to five. Do this several times until you start to feel the coordination of the tempo and the breath.

Then, sing the entire selection in tempo, taking silent, quick breaths where indicated. Be careful not to release the air when you rebreathe. This will help you to begin to create some muscle memory for breathing in silently and quickly.

If you feel yourself taking gaspy breaths, slow the tempo down until you can breathe in silently.

HOW CAN I KEEP FROM SINGING?

(breathe to five)
My life flows on in endless song'
above earth's lamentation.

(breathe to five)
I hear the sweet, though far-off hymn'
that greets a new creation.

(breathe to five)
Through all the mayhem and the strife'
I hear the music ringing.

(breathe to five)
It finds an echo in my heart.
How can I keep from singing?

Helpful Hints

As you become adept at rebreathing back to five, you may begin to notice a naturally occurring improvement in control of your breathing for singing. This exercise engages the abdominal muscles naturally and shows you how the management of pressurized air helps you to sing with a freely produced tone. The breathing muscles involved strengthen and create muscle memory, paving the way to singing longer phrases.

The Practice Room

Each day will begin each day with Exercise 7D to warm up your voice. Do not skip this exercise as it is an integral part of each day's Practice Plan. This will increase your practice session by approximately two minutes.

As written, these Practice Plans will now last an average of thirty minutes. Remember, it is not the quantity of time you practice, but the quality of the muscle movements that create results.

Practice Plan 10A

Practice Plan 10A focuses on the new breathing exercises and includes the song example at the end of each practice session.

Practice Plan 10B

Practice Plan 10B offers the practice song as an optional exercise after completing the day's tracks, which will add extra time to your practice session if you choose to use it.

Exercise 35

Singing the Hum

1. Speak the consonant combination "hnn" with a natural smiley stretch, making sure that the "h" begins the sound and that the "n" consonant sound originates with the tip of the tongue on the roof of the mouth just behind the front teeth.

2. Speak "hnn" again and then close your lips, changing the sound to the humming tone, "hmm" (with the "h" escaping through the nose).

3. Sing a single note on the consonant combination "hnn" with a natural smiley stretch. Make sure the "h" precedes the consonant "n" and that it originates

with the tip of the tongue on the roof of the mouth just behind the front teeth.

4. Release the note by stopping the breath. Relax the smile only after you have stopped the breath.

5. Sing "hnn" again, as described in step 1 above.

6. This time, while singing the "hnn," close your lips, changing the sound to the humming tone, "hmm," (the "h" will escape through the nose).

Referring to the instructions above, hum a five-note scale first on "hnn" and then on "hmm." Make sure to check your posture and breathe correctly before you begin. Remember to repeat each exercise a minimum of three times before moving to the next chord example.

Audio Tracks and Video: 35D, 35A, 35L, and 35V

hnn

hmm

Exercise 36

Learning the /hmm . . . mee/ Movement

In this exercise, you will combine the sounds "hmm" and /mee/ using the natural smiley stretch of the hum to set up an exaggerated pronunciation for the /ee/ vowel. The tendency is for the /ee/ vowel to sound nasal, but combining the hum and natural smiley stretch creates more space inside the acoustic chamber of the vocal tract, helping to improve the vocal sound.

For now, you must consciously stretch into the natural smiley position when practicing this exercise, with the intention of creating new muscle memory and habit. As you improve and the muscles become stronger and more flexible, you will replace the overt external smile with a slight lifting of the cheeks on the outside instead.

Be careful not to grip your lower jaw and front neck muscles when you pronounce the /ee/. This will happen if you show the lower teeth while pronouncing the /ee/. This presents itself as a very toothy smile that some people get in the habit of making

(I sometimes refer to it as the fashion model smile). This could negatively affect the correct position you need to create to sing the /ee/ properly.

If you do tend to show your bottom teeth for the /ee/ vowel, you will need to learn how to release your jaw. One way to do that is to sing the /ee/ with a slight overbite a few times until you feel the jaw release. Then cease the overbite and try the smiley stretch again. This usually takes care of the problem, but you may have to practice this for a while before it becomes completely comfortable.

You will learn this exercise faster if you practice in front of a mirror. Please watch the video of this exercise sequence to understand the muscle movements. You will speak this exercise as two separate syllables:

1. Stretch your facial muscles into a natural smiling position with your mouth slightly open and breathe in.

2. Begin the onset of the vocal sound by closing your mouth and speaking a "hmm" for at least one full beat.

3. Stop the "hmm" sound. Relax your lips.

4. Press your lips together to prepare the "m" consonant sound of the second syllable, /mee/.

5. Pronounce the "mm" sound and use the hum of the consonant sound "m" to stretch back into the smiley position while speaking an /ee/. This will produce the syllable /mee/.

6. Continue to stretch the muscles in the smiley position as you say /ee/, being careful not to tense the neck muscles.

7. Release the vowel with your breath but keep stretching your cheek muscles.

8. Relax your mouth.

9. Repeat this sequence until you can do it smoothly without having to look at the instructions. When you feel you can do this exercise correctly, proceed to Exercise 37.

hmm ...mee ...

Exercise 37

Connecting the /hmm/ and /mee/

The key to properly executing the connected version of this exercise is to continue the hum as you are preparing the consonant sound "m" to say /mee/. There are two separate smiley movements, one for the hum and another for the /mee/. Sometimes it helps if you think of this as a two-syllable word, /hmm—mee/. It is important to learn this exercise correctly before moving on, as it encourages a specific muscle pattern and coordination that occurs throughout the book.

Here is how you will connect the hum and the /mee/:

1. Stretch your facial muscles into the natural smiley stretch position with your mouth slightly open and breathe in.

2. Begin the onset of the vocal sound by closing your mouth and, as you speak the hum, stretch your smiling muscles. Speak the "hmm" for at least one full beat.

3. Continue voicing the hum but, as you do, relax your lip and cheek muscles.

4. Press your lips together to pronounce the "m" and then use the consonant sound to stretch your muscles into the natural smiley stretch position to speak the /ee/ vowel. This will produce the syllable /mee/.

5. Continue to stretch the muscles in the smiley position as you say /ee/.

6. Release the vowel with your breath.

7. Relax the natural smiley stretch.

Repeat steps 1–7 four more times, speaking them as indicated below:

Audio Track and Video: 37S and 37V

hmm . . .mee / hmm . . .mee / hmm . . .mee / hmm . . .mee / hmm . . .mee

Exercise 38

Sung Separated /hmm . . . mee/

The key to properly executing the connected version of this exercise is to continue the hum as you are preparing the consonant sound "m" to say /mee/. There are two separate smiley movements, one for the hum and another for the /mee/. Sometimes it helps if you think of this as a two-syllable word, /hmm—mee/. It is important to learn this exercise correctly before moving on, as it encourages a specific muscle pattern and coordination that occurs throughout the book.

Sing this exercise slowly in front of a mirror, checking to make sure you consistently stretch to the natural smiley stretch position.

Remember to repeat each exercise a minimum of three times before moving to the next chord example.

1. Stretch your facial muscles into the natural smiley stretch position, with your mouth slightly open, and breathe to five.

2. Begin the onset of the vocal sound by closing your mouth as you sing the hum and stretching your smiling muscles. Sing the "hmm" for at least one full beat.

3. Continue voicing the hum but, as you do, relax your lip and cheek muscles.

4. Press your lips together to pronounce the "m" and then use the consonant sound "m" to stretch your muscles into the smiley position to sing the /ee/ vowel. This will produce the syllable /mee/.

5. Continue to stretch the muscles in the smiley position as you sing /ee/.

6. Release the vowel with your breath.

7. Relax the natural smiley stretch.

8. Repeat steps 1–7 four more times.

Audio and Video Tracks: 38D, 38A, 38L, and Video 38V

hmm...mee   hmm...mee   hmm...mee   hmm...mee   hmm...mee

THE PRACTICE ROOM

As written, these Practice Plans will now last an average of twenty-five to thirty minutes. Your voice teacher or vocal coach may choose to omit one or two tracks if you need a shorter practice session. Be careful not to leave out any track numbers that you learned this week, though. Remember, it is not the quantity of time you practice, but the quality of the muscle movements that create results.

- Check your posture.

- Breathe to five before you sing.

- Use a mirror to check your form.

Both plans include exercises 35-38 where you learned to connect and sing the / hmm . . . mee/ movement.

Practice Plan 11A

This Practice Plan will begin with humming practice followed by the /hmm ... mee/ movement exercises to reinforce the concepts learned in this lesson and to warm up your voice for the rest of the exercises. Do not skip these daily exercises, as they are an integral part of creating muscle memory for the vowel /ee/.

Practice Plan 11B

You can follow this Practice Plan once you have completed 11A.

Exercise 39

Spoken Connected /hmm . . . mee/

To connect the /mee/ sounds, begin with a strong hum and follow it with five /mee/ syllables. Your lips and facial muscles will move back and forth between the mouth position of the consonant "m," and the /ee/ vowel.

Remember to smile again on every syllable! This exercise engages the cheek muscles in particular to aid in the development of flexibility and strength in the face. Make sure to add a hum to the first /mee/ syllable to reinforce the natural smiley stretch.

Audio Track and Video: 39S and 39V

hmm . . . mee_mee_mee_mee_mee__

Exercise 40

Sung Connected /hmm . . . mee_mee/

As in the spoken exercise, remember to smile on every syllable! This exercise engages the cheek muscles in particular to aid in the development of flexibility and strength in the face. Make sure to add a hum to the first /mee/ syllable to reinforce the natural smiley stretch.

Sing this five-note-scale exercise slowly in front of a mirror, checking to make sure you are consistently stretching back to the smiley position. Remember to repeat each exercise a minimum of three times before moving to the next chord example.

Audio Tracks and Video: 40D, 40A, and 40V

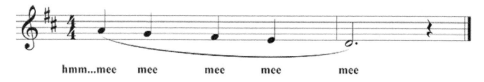

hmm...mee   mee   mee   mee   mee

Exercise 41

Bent Cries on /hmm . . . mee/

You will begin with a series of bent cries to initiate a proper stretch inside your mouth. You will sing the pitch and then bend it a bit. Use the hum at the beginning of the cry to help establish the vocalization. This will feel similar to the beginning of Exercise 38, /hmm . . . mee/.

Remember that cries are a combination of elongated speech and easy calling, as in the phrases "Hey, wait! Wait for me!" Sing cries at a medium volume but with a gentle stretch that releases the voice, allowing it to cry out. There are numerous examples of cries on the exercise tracks, and they are there to help you learn how to make the best cry possible.

Although the exercise pattern only indicates the singing of two bent cries, when you are learning this initially you may need to sing several more before attempting the third cry. The idea is to train your muscles in this new movement so that the third cry will integrate that form.

When you do sing the third cry, move quickly across the interval of the fifth. This allows the muscles to learn to navigate the movement without trying to control the speed of a slower cry. Be careful, though, that you do not skip to the bottom note of the cry. If you find that you are skipping, take a few moments and do some sirens up and down the range of your voice to help you find that type of vocalization. As mentioned before, you may need to tap into some silliness here and imitate the sound of a fire truck! Or, you can sing the first note of the fifth cry for two beats before starting the cry, to give yourself a little time to prepare mentally.

Remember to repeat each exercise a minimum of three times before moving to the next chord example.

1. Stretch your facial muscles into a natural smiley stretch with your mouth slightly open.

2. Breathe through your mouth to five and begin the onset of the vocal sound by closing your mouth as you sing the hum and stretching your smiling muscles. Sing the "hmm" for at least one full beat.

3. Continue singing the hum but, as you do, relax your lip and cheek muscles.

4. Press your lips together to pronounce the "m," use the consonant sound "m" to stretch into the smiling position, and sing the /ee/ vowel, bending it a bit.

5. Continue to stretch the muscles as you sing the bent /ee/ vowel.

6. Release the vowel with your breath but continue to invoke the natural smiley stretch. You may hear or feel a slight "y" sound at the end, which indicates that you are stretching and bending the pitch correctly.

7. Relax the natural smiley stretch.

8. Repeat steps 1–8 two more times.

Audio Tracks and Video: 41D, 41A, and 41V

hmm...mee_____   hmm...mee_____   hmm...mee_____

Exercise 42

Cries in Fifths on /hmm . . . mee/

It is vitally important to breathe to five as you practice the cries and to avoid holding your breath. Make sure that you stretch through the cry, avoid locking the cheek muscles, and, when you reach the last pitch, sing it completely and release the breath properly, remembering to continue the stretch until after the release.

This exercise is a variation of Exercise 41, but excludes the bent cry. The goal for this exercise is to be able to start the cry immediately and sing the glide bit longer over the interval of the fifth. Do not worry if you are unable to accomplish this right away. It may take some time to get the coordination of the fifth cries, but they will improve with deliberate practicing, and eventually they will become a part of your standard repertoire of vocal exercises.

You will start this exercise by emphasizing the hum in front of the /ee/ vowel, which is followed by a strong /mee/ syllable. Focus on practicing these cries in your medium and low range to assist in strengthening the natural smiley stretch for this vowel.

1. Move your facial muscles into the natural smiley stretch position with your mouth slightly open.

2. Breathe through your mouth to five, and begin the onset of the vocal sound by closing your mouth as you sing the hum, while stretching your smiling muscles. Sing the "hmm" for at least one full beat.

3. Continue singing the hum but, as you do, relax your lip and cheek muscles.

4. Press your lips together to pronounce the "m," use the consonant sound "m" to stretch into the smiling position, and sing the /ee/ vowel.

5. As you glide through the interval of a fifth, continue to stretch the muscles

6. as you sing, extending the /ee/ cry to the bottom note.

7. Release the vowel with your breath. You may hear or feel a slight "y" sound at the end, which indicates that you are stretching and bending the pitch correctly.

8. Relax the natural smiley stretch.

Audio Tracks: 42D and 42A

hmm...mee

Here are some things to remember:

- It is vitally important to avoid holding your breath as you initiate the cries.

- As you glide through the cry, continue to invoke the natural smiley stretch.

- When you reach the last pitch, sing it completely, release it properly, and continue stretching until after you release the breath.

- Make sure you are observing and adjusting your mouth movements with a mirror.

- Remember to repeat each exercise a minimum of three times before moving to the next chord example.

Helpful Hints

The /ee/ vowel is naturally a nasal vowel, requiring strong articulation by the tongue. However, if sung properly, with a lift inside of the mouth, the vowel will have a warmer sound. Sound waves that travel into the nasal passages tend to maintain higher frequencies that we perceive as nasality or twang, and singing with a natural smiley stretch helps to eliminate some of those nasal overtones.

This is helpful information to know if you sing CCM, as those styles often use or desire a nasal tone quality. In that case, you will train your voice so that you can create both tonal sounds, but you will focus first on the development of a strong warm /ee/ sound. That will give you a strong foundational tone on which you can impose nasality to whatever degree you need. Having the ability to change the quality of your voice like this gives you a larger palette of sounds you can use to express yourself through your singing. The imposition of nasality on a warm foundational tone also gives a nice overall underpinning to the vocal quality of the singer.

131

THE PRACTICE ROOM

As written, these Practice Plans will now last an average of thirty minutes. Your voice teacher of vocal coach may choose to omit one or two tracks if you need a shorter practice session. Be careful not to leave out any track numbers that you learned this week, though. Remember, it is not the quantity of time you practice, but the quality of the muscle movements that create results.

- Check your posture.

- Breathe to five before you sing.

- Use a mirror to check your form.

Practice Plan 12A

Practice Plan 12B

These Practice Plans contain the cry exercises as presented in exercises 39-42.

Remember to begin with a strong hum and follow it with the /mee/ syllables in these exercises and to smile again on every syllable! These exercises engage the cheek muscles in particular to aid in the development of flexibility and strength in the face.

When practicing the cries, start the cry immediately and sing the glide bit longer over the interval of the fifth. Do not worry if you are unable to accomplish this right away. It may take some time to get the coordination of the fifth cries, but they will improve with deliberate practicing, and eventually they will become a part of your standard repertoire of vocal exercises.

Exercise 43

Breathe after Three on /hmm . . . mee/

Remember, the intention of these "Breathe after Three" exercises is to make you breathe early after only singing three notes. This interrupting-breath exercise will begin to teach you how it feels to naturally refill the lungs while maintaining a cushion of air in your lungs. As you become more competent, you will be able to sing in tempo, and the breathing will become quicker.

1. Breathe to five.

2. Breathe after the third note. It is okay to interrupt the tempo of this exercise to refill the lungs. Take time to breathe back to five after the third note.

3. Do not hold your breath before singing!

4. Allow the air to flow into your body when you take the second breath. There is no trick to this; simply inhale again slowly to five. Take your time!

Remember to repeat each exercise a minimum of three times before moving to the next chord example.

Audio Track: 43D and 43A

hmm...mee   mee_____

Exercise 44: Responsive Breathing on /yoo/
Exercise 45: Responsive Breathing on /yoh/

These new exercises are a variation on Exercise 32, Breathe after Three, from chapter 8, and they will help you experience the way the ribs and the intercostal muscles stay active while you are singing. They contain three additional note patterns, with a pause in between to take a breath.

Remember to repeat each exercise a minimum of three times before moving to the next chord example.

1. Breathe to five and sing the first three notes slowly. Remember to stretch your lips through the legato phrase.

2. Without collapsing your ribs, silently breathe in enough air to replenish what you exhaled singing the three notes in step 1.

3. Sing the next two notes slowly and evenly.

4. Breathe to five again, silently refilling the exhaled air without collapsing the ribs.

5. Continue in this manner to the end of the exercise.

Audio Tracks /yoo/: 44D and 44A
Audio Tracks /yoh/: 45D and 45A

44   yoo _____   yoo ____   yoo ____   yoo ____   yoo _____

45   yoh _____   yoh ____   yoh ____   yoh ____   yoh _____

The key to singing these exercises correctly is learning how to allow the air back into your lungs when you rebreathe. Specifically, you will need to resist the inclination to hold your breath after you stop singing the first three notes, because that closes the vocal cords.

Another common mistake is to relax and exhale, which collapses the rib position. The following sequence demonstrates the correct breathing pattern for these exercises:

1. Breathe to five.

2. Sing.

3. Breathe and refill to five, allowing the air back into your lungs.

4. Sing.

5. Breathe and refill to five, allowing the air back into your lungs.

6. Sing.

7. Breathe and refill to five, allowing the air back into your lungs.

8. Sing.

9. Breathe and refill to five, allowing the air back into your lungs.

10. Sing.

11. Release.

THE PRACTICE ROOM

Please remember that as written, Practice Plans 11 through 16 are an average length of twenty-five to thirty minutes. Your voice teacher of vocal coach may choose to omit one or two tracks if you need a shorter practice session. Be careful not to leave out any track numbers that you learned this week, though. Remember, it is not the quantity of time you practice, but the quality of the muscle movements that create results.

Practice Plan 13A

Practice Plan 13B

These interrupting-breath exercises will begin to teach you how it feels to naturally refill the lungs while maintaining a cushion of air in your lungs. As you become more competent, you will be able to sing in tempo, and the breathing will become more responsive.

Exercise 46: Breathe Every Three on /whoo/

Exercise 47: Breathe Every Three on /whoh/

Regardless of the confusion caused by trying to control the diaphragm's movements (i.e., improperly tensing the abdominal muscles), we absolutely do want the diaphragm muscle to have bounce and flexibility as it aids in the exhalation of air across the vocal cords. It is very important at this point in your breathing study to become an observer of all of the muscles involved in breath management, as their movement will inform you how the respiratory system is working while you sing.

We will continue with another variation on the previous breathing exercises by lengthening the singing portion of the exercise and adding a sequence of three notes. Breathe Every Three exercises are made up of a five-note scale in a down-up-down pattern, and you will interrupt the phrase by refilling your breath every three notes.

This exercise helps your body learn how to manage the frequent breaths that might occur in a song by isolating them in a similarly patterned exercise that encourages the natural renewing of the breath and creates a slight natural bounce in the diaphragm and abdominal region. Please note that at this point in study you will work the middle and low range of the voice for successful employment of both breathing to five and the execution of renewing breaths successfully.

1. Breathe to five and sing the first three notes slowly. Remember to stretch your lips forward through the legato phrase.

2. Without collapsing your ribs, silently breathe in enough air to replenish what you exhaled singing the three notes in step 1.

3. Sing the next three notes slowly and evenly, initiating the vowel with the consonant sound "wh" for vowel sounds /oo/ and /oh/.

4. Breathe again, silently refilling the exhaled air without collapsing the ribs.

5. Continue in this manner to the end of the exercise.

Remember to repeat each exercise a minimum of three times before moving to the next chord example.

Audio Tracks /whoo/: 46D and 46A

Audio Tracks /whoh/: 47D and 47A

THE PRACTICE ROOM

Please remember that as written, Practice Plans 11 through 16 are an average length of twenty-five to thirty minutes. Your voice teacher of vocal coach may choose to omit one or two tracks if you need a shorter practice session. Be careful not to leave out any track numbers that you learned this week, though. Remember, it is not the quantity of time you practice, but the quality of the muscle movements that create results.

Practice Plan 14A

Practice Plan 14B

Practice Plan 14C

These interrupting-breath exercises continue to teach you how it feels to naturally refill the lungs while maintaining a cushion of air in your lungs. It is very important at this point in your breathing study to become an observer of all of the muscles involved in breath management, as their movement will inform you how the respiratory system is working while you sing.

Exercise 48

Producing the Spoken kh Sound

1. Breathe to five.

2. Stretch your mouth into a smile and speak three *k* consonants in a row. It will create a percussive and short hissing sound. Do not use your vocal cords to pronounce the consonant or you will end up with a /g/ sound.

3. As long as this exercise does not make you feel light-headed, repeat it two more times. Do not do any more than three repetitions, as the exercise uses a lot of air, and you do not want to become dizzy.

$$k—k—k—$$

Next, you will add some hissing to the k sound.

1. Breathe to five.

2. Make a natural smiley stretch with your mouth.

3. Speak the k sound slowly, three times in a row, allowing some air to escape as you say the k.

4. If you are doing this correctly, you will feel your tongue strongly press against the inside of your upper molars, and against the roof of your mouth, with extra air escaping across your tongue and out your mouth. As you work through these exercises, you will experience a fair amount of hiss, which is desirable.

5. As long as this exercise does not make you feel light-headed, do it three times. Do not do any more than three repetitions, as the exercise uses a lot of air, and you do not want to become dizzy.

Audio Track: 48S

kh kh kh

Exercise 49

Spoken Separated Extended khhhhh Sound

This exercise extends the amount of hissing after the articulation of the kh.

1. Breathe to five.

2. Make a natural smiley stretch with your mouth.

3. Begin by speaking two khh sounds followed by a third khhhhh with a lot of additional hiss at the end. Try to prolong the hissing sound for two beats so you can feel the strength of the tongue in this articulation.

4. Be sure to pronounce the khhhhh consonant fully.

5. As long as this exercise does not make you feel light-headed, repeat it two more times. Do not do any more than three repetitions, as the exercise uses a lot of air, and you do not want to become dizzy.

Audio Track: 49S and 49V

khh khh khhhhh

Exercise 50

Spoken Separated /khhee/

Now you will combine the khh sound and the /ee/ vowel to produce the /khhee/ syllable.

1. Breathe to five.

2. Stretch your mouth into a natural smiley stretch and speak the short percussive khh followed by the /ee/ vowel: /khhee/. This will sound like you are speaking the word key.

3. Next, repeat this syllable two more times, separating each syllable. If you are doing this correctly, your mouth will move into a natural smiley stretch position for each syllable.

138

4. As long as this exercise does not make you feel light-headed, repeat it two more times. Do not do any more than three repetitions, as the exercise uses a lot of air, and you do not want to become dizzy.

Audio Track: 50S

/khhee/ /khhee/ /khhee/

Exercise 51

Removing the *k* from the khhhhh Sound

This is the exercise where you will learn how to transition from the khhhhh sound to a hhhhhh sound.

1. Breathe to five.

2. Stretch your mouth into a natural smiley stretch and speak the extended /khhhhh/ syllable.

3. Speak the extended hhhhhh portion of the syllable without the *k*.

4. Speak this sequence three times, alternating between khhhhh and hhhhhh.

5. As long as this sequence does not make you feel light-headed, repeat it two more times. Do not do any more than three repetitions, as the exercise uses a lot of air, and you do not want to become dizzy.

Audio Track: 51S

khhhhh hhhhhh khhhhh hhhhhh khhhhh

Exercise 52

Spoken Separated /hmm . . . mee hhhhhhee/

Begin speaking the first syllable with a hum to help to initiate a more effective natural smiley stretch.

1. Breathe to five.

2. Stretch your mouth into a natural smiley stretch and speak the /hmm...mee/ syllable.

3. Speak the extended hhhhhh consonant, and allow the /ee/ vowel to emanate from it as you move your mouth into the natural smiley stretch.

Audio Track: 52S

hmm . . . mee_ hhhhhee_hhhhhee_hhhhhee_ hhhhhee___

Exercise 53

Sung Separated /hmm . . . mee/ plus /hhhhhhee/

1. Breathe to five.

2. Begin singing the first syllable with a hum, which will help to initiate a more effective natural smiley stretch.

3. When you initiate the /hhhhhhee/, spend as much time as possible pronouncing the hhhhhh, and allow the /ee/ vowel to emanate from it.

You may want to rebreathe to five between each note and take your time with each pitch.

Audio Track: 53D and 53A

hmm...mee   hhhhhhee   hhhhhhee   hhhhhhee   hhhhhhee

Exercise 54

Connected /hmm . . . mee/ plus /khhee/ or /hhhhhhee/

Next, you will take the articulations you learned in the previous exercises and connect them together with a faster tempo.

1. Breathe to five.

2. Begin singing the first syllable with a hum, which will help to initiate a more effective natural smiley stretch, followed by the /ee/ vowel.

3. Sing the rest of the exercise on /khhee/.

4. Sing the exercise again, but substitute the /khee/ syllable with the /hhhhhhee/ syllable while connecting the syllables together.

5. Sing this exercise at a moderate tempo, keeping the rhythm and tempo consistent and even as demonstrated in the audio track.

Audio Tracks: 54D, 54A and 54V

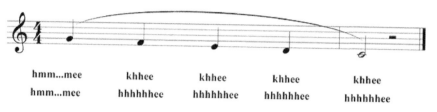

| hmm...mee | khhee | khhee | khhee | khhee |
| hmm...mee | hhhhhhee | hhhhhhee | hhhhhhee | hhhhhhee |

Using strong consonant articulation helps you improve vocal production by exercising the muscles, solidifying mouth positions, and creating muscle memory that supports a consistent tone. Once that is in place, intentional thinking of vowels and consonants helps to move the voice in a manner that creates a smooth-sounding vocal sound, also known as *vocal line.*

Remember, these exercises are a means to an end, as they introduce you to a better understanding of what an active mouth feels like while at the same time strengthening the articulation of your tongue for the /ee/ vowel.

HELPFUL HINTS

Using strong consonant articulation helps you improve vocal production by exercising the muscles, solidifying mouth positions, and creating muscle memory that supports a consistent tone. Once that is in place, intentional thinking of vowels and consonants helps to move the voice in a manner that creates a smooth-sounding vocal sound, also known as vocal line.

THE PRACTICE ROOM

Please remember that Practice Plans 15 and 16 will now last an average of thirty minutes. Your voice teacher of vocal coach may choose to omit one or two tracks if you need a shorter practice session. Be careful not to leave out any track numbers that you learned this week, though. Remember, it is not the quantity of time you practice, but the quality of the muscle movements that create results.

Make sure to do the following activities during this week's Practice Plan:

- Check your posture.

- Breathe to five before you sing. Do not collapse between breaths but breathe in to replace the air used.

- Continue to use a mirror to check your form.

Practice Plan 15A

Practice Plan 15B

These Practice Plans introduce the concept of the spoken percussive "kh" sound as presented in exercises 48-51. All of these exercises are short in length, but you need to attain a degree of competency in each before moving ahead to the next one.

Remember, these exercises are a means to an end, as they introduce you to a better understanding of what an active mouth feels like while at the same time strengthening the articulation of your tongue for the /ee/ vowel.

Practice Plan 16A

Practice Plan 16B

These Practice Plans replace the percussive "kh" sound with the "hhhhhh" consonant pattern, as presented in exercises 52-54. Although these exercises are somewhat challenging, you will need to spend some time working through the internal articulation as it will strengthen your ability to produce a better vocal tone.

Exercise 55

Responsive Breathing on /mee hee/

Using the consonant *h* to help with articulation is a means to an end. Eventually, all of the exercises and songs you sing where you might use an *h* in practice will disappear as you learn to initiate any open vowel without the assistance of consonants, except of course, for those words that actually begin with *h*!

This is not the strong hhhhhh consonant of previous exercises, although your experience articulating that consonant grouping should make this consonant h much easier to sing.

1. Breathe to five and sing the first three notes slowly. Remember to use a natural smiley stretch throughout the legato phrase.

2. Without collapsing your ribs, silently breathe in enough air to replenish what you exhaled when singing the three notes in step 1.

3. Sing the next two notes slowly and evenly, initiating the vowel with the consonant h.

4. Breathe again, silently refilling the exhaled air without collapsing the ribs.

5. Continue in this manner to the end of the exercise.

Audio Tracks: 55D and 55A

Exercise 56

Breathe Every Three on /mee hee/

Breathe Every Three exercises are made up of a five-note scale in a down-up-down pattern. You will interrupt the phrase by refilling your breath every three notes.

1. Breathe to five and sing the first three notes slowly. Remember to use a natural smiley stretch through the legato phrase.

2. Without collapsing your ribs, silently breathe in enough air to replenish what you exhaled when singing the three notes in step 1.

3. Sing the next three notes slowly, initiating the vowel with the consonant h.

4. Breathe again, silently refilling the exhaled air without collapsing the ribs.

5. Continue in this manner to the end of the exercise.

Audio Tracks: 56D and 56A

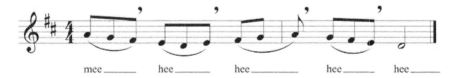

Exercise 57

Introducing Legato Singing Using a Silent Consonant Articulation

We certainly can agree that your thoughts control the movement of your muscles. You think to yourself, I am going to pick up that pencil, and you reach over and pick up the pencil. It is rather amazing, when you think of it (pun intended). Since muscle movement produces vocal production, it would follow that we can think our muscles into vocal actions. The only difference in singing is that you cannot see the results.

So, how do you think your way through your singing? Practice and focus. This may seem like a crazy idea at the outset, but it is strongly rooted in physiology. Without going into all of the scientific, neural, and anatomical movements, suffice to say that your brain controls your muscles, and your muscles will pretty much do what you think. That is the easy part to understand. *The hard part is practicing that approach.* You will learn about this in the next exercise, but it has a quirky instruction: You must simply engage your thoughts to sing!

The secret to learning how to sing the smooth legato exercise is to think a strong *h* (indicated by the symbol hhhhhh) on each note.

1. *Thinking* a strong consonant sound will slightly engage and activate the tongue, helping with articulation and creating the vocal onset with air.

2. You will keep the energy going between the notes by thinking of the pronunciation of the hhhhhh in front of the vowel.

3. Remember, you are *not* actually pronouncing the hhhhhh consonant aloud *just thinking it!*

4. Be sure to continue the natural smiley stretch throughout the entire scale.

Audio Track: 57D

hmm...mee

Exercise 58

Legato Using Silent Vowel Articulation

Our next exercise is similar to the previous one with the goal of singing a sustained legato on a /hmm . . . mee/ syllable. This time you will think about pronouncing a pure /ee/ vowel sound for each pitch. This is similar to the previous exercise, but it will show you that thinking the vowel actually tells the muscles to move to that position and sets in motion an environment for good acoustic resonance. However, the task is not only to think, as it is vitally important to stretch constantly through the smile as you sing this exercise.

Some singers, in their attempts to do the exercise correctly, will overcompensate and lock the natural smiley stretch instead of stretching through the cheek muscles. Others will fail to stretch enough through the duration of the exercise and risk locking the tongue. Obviously, you should avoid locking any muscle while singing, which can cause an ugly erk sound in the tone.

To avoid locking, think about initiating a natural smiley stretch on each note while thinking about the /ee/ vowel. In other words, you will sing five vowels on five notes, thinking about each one as you go.

1. *Thinking* the vowel sound will slightly engage and activate the tongue, helping with articulation and creating the vocal onset with air.

2. You will keep the energy going between the notes, by rethinking the /ee/ for each pitch of the scale.

3. Remember, you are *not* physically pronouncing the vowel aloud *just thinking it!*

Audio Track: 58D

Moving your muscles with your thoughts is not limited to singing vocal exercises. Once you become more proficient at *thinking* your way through these exercises, you can start to apply them to your songs. Keeping in mind that the quality of our vowels

145

determines our vocal tone, try thinking more about the vowels of your words as you are singing your songs. This will also make you aware of how to think ahead while you are singing, much in the same way you form your sentences before you speak. This helps you to have a more natural communication with your audience.

Exercise 59

Cry and Legato Scale on /hmm . . . mee/

The following exercise encourages the stretch of the cry for the production of a five-note descending scale. The beauty of the cry exercise is that it helps set up the mouth for the kind of active stretching that is needed to sing a clean legato scale.

By now, you should be familiar enough with the concept of thinking your muscles into position to try the following:

1. Establish the hum and /ee/ as in the two previous exercises

2. Sing the cry, focusing the stretch and releasing properly.

3. Establish the hum and sing the first note of the scale.

4. As you think about the articulation of each /ee/ vowel, actively maintain the stretchy position of the cry. (Refer to Exercise 58 for more information.)

Audio Tracks and Video: 59D, 59A, and 59V

hmm...mee_____   hmm...mee_____

THE PRACTICE ROOM

Warm-Up and Warm-Down Exercises

From now on, you will begin each practice session using two well-known exercises: the 7D Connected /yoo/ Scale and the 18A Connected /yoh/ Scale. These are the exercises I use in my studio to warm up students at the beginning of their lessons. The forward stretch of the /oo/ helps to open up the low range, and the more open interior of the /oh/ is great for warming up the higher range.

Additionally, there is a humming exercise at the end of each practice session. I encourage students to include this, regardless of the length of your practice session. The hum gives the voice an opportunity to release the muscles. Some would call this a warm-down exercise. Although there has been very little research on the benefits of a warm down, logically it makes sense, and it does feel good at the end of a practice session to end with some humming. You may hum with or without the natural smiley stretch, whatever feels best for your voice.

There is one very important change for singing the warm-up and warm-down exercises (7D, 18A, 35L, and 35D). You will only sing one repetition per chord example:

1. Press Play. The piano chord sounds, followed by the sung example.

2. Press Pause.

3. Sing the example once.

4. Press Play.

5. Continue singing the exercise with one repetition per chord example.

Increase in Practice Time

Practice Plans 17A and 17B increase the number of tracks to seven or eight a day. Your voice teacher of vocal coach may choose to omit one or two tracks if you need a shorter practice session. Be careful not to leave out any track numbers that you learned this week, though. Remember, it is not the quantity of time you practice, but the quality of the muscle movements that create results.

By this point in the book, you should be practicing twenty to thirty minutes per day, five days a week. If you are practicing thirty minutes per day, feel free to break up your practicing into smaller segments of ten or fifteen minutes each.

Practice Plan 17A

Practice Plan 17B

Practice Plan 17A shows you the design of the Warm-Up, Practice, and Warm-Down sections. This is the only time you will find it in this format. The rest of the Practice Plans will only list the tracks in their regular practicing order.

147

OTHER HELPFUL HINTS

Moving your muscles with your thoughts is not limited to singing vocal exercises. Once you become more proficient at thinking your way through the exercises in this chapter, you can start to apply them to your songs. Keeping in mind that the quality of our vowels determines our vocal tone, try thinking more about the vowels of your words as you are singing your songs. This will also make you aware of how to think ahead while you are singing, much in the same way you form your sentences before you speak. This helps you to have a more natural communication with your audience. Using strong consonant articulation helps you to improve vocal production by exercising the muscles, solidifying mouth positions, and creating the muscle memory to support a consistent tone. Once that is in place, intentionally thinking about the vowels and consonants helps to move the voice in a manner that creates vocal line.

Exercise 60

Spoken Vowel Transitions

The following exercise will help you to understand the progression of the vowel sounds as they present themselves in the mouth for the following words:

fleece - face - kit - dress - trap - palm - strut - goat - goose

Vowel sounds derived from the above key words:

ee — ā — ĭ — eh — ă — ah — uh — oh — oo

Say each vowel sound slowly (not the words), pausing in between each but still dragging out each vowel sound. You will notice that your tongue and mouth positions change slightly for each sound, starting from a broad natural smiley stretch with the /ee/ and ending in a pursed forward lip position with the /oo/.

Audio Track: 60S

ee—ā—ĭ—eh—ă—ah—uh—oh—oo

The Natural Smiley Stretch and Pursed Lips

Now speak the vowel sounds (not the words), but connect them while continuing the stretch of the smile for all of the vowels indicated in the chart below and pursing your lips for the last two vowel sounds, /oh-oo/. This may feel a bit awkward, but you should notice a stronger tone emerge for each sound produced with the stronger mouth positions.

148

Key words:

Invoke the Natural Smiley Stretch	Purse Lips
fleece - face - kit - dress - trap - palm - strut	goat - goose
ee___ā___ĭ_eh___ă__ah__uh	oh___oo

You might find it a little bit challenging to maintain the natural smiley stretch on the vowel sounds of /ah/ and /uh/. The tendency is to pronounce them in their mouth position without the natural smiley stretch. Although this position may seem somewhat awkward, keep in mind that we are giving the muscles a workout, not trying to develop exact vowel positions.

Exercise 61
Separated /bah/ as in Palm

This exercise introduces the consonant sound b, which helps you spring your muscles into the natural smiley stretch for the /ah/ vowel. The consonant b belongs to a group of consonants called plosives, because when pronouncing them, air pressure builds up behind your closed lips and then explodes when the lips release.

It is also a voiced consonant, since the vocal cords are involved in the production of the sound. Conversely, b has a silent plosive consonant partner, with no vocal cord contribution. That voiceless (or unvoiced) consonant is p. The consonants b and p are just one of a number of pairs of voiced/unvoiced consonants you will encounter as you continue through these exercises.

As you sing the /ah/, you may feel that the position of the tongue is a bit lower than the /ee/ vowel, which is the only other natural smiley stretch vowel you have learned. You will probably feel a bit of space naturally open up in the back of your mouth, but you should not try to change anything or enhance that space. Just observe it and make sure that you use the natural smiley stretch to get the best vocal tone possible.

1. Breathe to five slowly and silently through your mouth.

2. Press and hold your lips together for a moment to prepare the pronunciation of the consonant b.

3. As the b explodes, use that energy to assist with moving your cheek musc
into the natural smiley stretch and then sing the /ah/.

4. Continue to invoke the natural smiley stretch while you sing the /ah/.

5. Release the vowel with your breath.

6. Relax your mouth but do not collapse your breath. Simply inhale and prep;
for the next syllable.

7. Take your time between each syllable to prepare your mouth properly. At t
point, do not worry about singing this exercise in tempo.

Audio Track: 61D and 61A

bah   bah   bah   bah   bah

Exercise 62

Spoken Connected /hmm . . . mah_mah/

The next exercise is good for muscle flexibility, but you must be careful not to si
it too quickly. Pay attention to the stretching from the m consonant on each pitch, a
use that momentum to launch the vowel. Start the hmm with a natural smiley stret
and allow the humming to help engage the onset of the vowel sounds wherever
occurs in the exercise.

Before singing this exercise, you will speak connected /hmm . . . ma
sounds. As with Exercise 39S, begin with a strong hum followed by fi
/hmm . . . mah/ syllables. Your lips and facial muscles will move back and forth b
tween the mouth position of the consonant m and the /ah/ vowel.

Audio Track: 62S

hmm. . . mah__mah__mah__mah__mah

Exercise 63

Sung Connected /hmm . . . mah_mah/

Sing the following exercise by using the muscle movements you learned in the previous spoken exercise. Remember to smile again on every syllable! This exercise engages the cheek muscles in particular to aid in the development of flexibility and strength in the face. Make sure to add a hum to the first /hmm . . . mah/ syllable to reinforce the natural smiley stretch. Sing this five-note-scale exercise slowly in front of a mirror, checking to make sure you are consistently stretching back to the natural smiley stretch position.

Audio Track: 63D and 63A

hmm...mah   mah   mah   mah   mah ____

Exercise 64

Separated /dā/ as in Face

This exercise introduces the consonant-vowel pair /dā/. The d is a dental-stop consonant, articulated with your tongue behind your upper teeth and stopping the flow of air. It is a voiced consonant and has an unvoiced partner, t.

Make sure that you create enough vocal sound when pronouncing the d to distinguish it from a t. An easy way to encourage a stronger sound is to allow the tip of your tongue to linger on the roof of your mouth while you are voicing the consonant. The longer you linger, the stronger your articulation will become. Try it a few times slowly and gradually build up the speed of the pronunciation of the d.

1. Breathe to five slowly and silently through your mouth.

2. Press and lightly hold your tongue on the roof of your mouth just behind your front teeth for a moment to initiate the consonant d.

3. Use the energy from pronouncing the d to assist your cheek muscles to move into the natural smiley stretch and sing the /ā/.

4. Continue to invoke the natural smiley stretch while you sing the /ā/.

5. Release the vowel with your breath.

6. Relax your mouth but do not collapse your breath. Simply inhale and prepare for the next syllable.

Audio Track: 64D and 64A

dā   dā   dā   dā   dā

Exercise 65

Spoken Connected /hmm . . . mā_mā/

Before singing this exercise, you will practice speaking connected /mā/ sounds. As with the previous exercise, begin with a strong hum followed by five /mā/ syllables. Your lips and facial muscles will move back and forth between the mouth position of the consonant m and the /ā/ vowel.

Audio Track: 65S

hmm . . . mā_mā_mā_mā_mā____

Exercise 66

Sung Connected /hmm . . . mā_mā/

Sing the following exercise by using the muscle movements you learned in the previous spoken exercise. Remember to smile again on every syllable! This exercise engages the cheek muscles in particular to aid in the development of flexibility and strength in the face. Make sure to add a hum to the first /mā/ syllable to reinforce the natural smiley stretch.

Sing this five-note-scale exercise slowly in front of a mirror, checking to make sure you are consistently stretching back to the natural smiley stretch position.

Audio Track: 66D and 66A

hmm...mā   mā   mā   mā   mā____

THE PRACTICE ROOM

Please remember that the first two tracks, 7D, 18A, and the last, 35D or 35A, are there to warm up and warm down your voice, and you should always include these in your practicing. Your voice teacher of vocal coach may choose to omit one or two tracks if you need a shorter practice session. Be careful not to leave out any track numbers that you learned this week, though. Remember, it is not the quantity of time you practice, but the quality of the muscle movements that create results.

Practice Plan 18A

The /ah/ Vowel

As you sing the /ah/, you may feel that the position of the tongue is a bit lower than the /ee/ vowel, which is the only other natural smiley stretch vowel you have learned. You will probably feel a bit of space naturally open up in the back of your mouth, but you should not try to change anything or enhance that space. Just observe it and make sure that you use the natural smiley stretch to get the best vocal tone possible.

Practice Plan 18B

The /ā/ Vowel

Remember that when you sing the separated /dā/ exercise, make sure to create enough vocal sound when pronouncing the "d" to distinguish it from a "t." An easy way to encourage a stronger sound is to allow the tip of your tongue to linger on the roof of your mouth while you are voicing the consonant. The longer you linger, the stronger your articulation will become. Try it a few times slowly and gradually build up the speed of the pronunciation of the "d."

Practice Plan 18C

The /ā/ and /ah/ Vowels

It is important for you to remember that you will use simple mouth positions for the low to medium-high part of the vocal range. This is a short-term strategy to encourage strong, exaggerated articulation in the mouth. Once your muscles are stronger and more flexible and your mouth is more active, the external stretching will diminish significantly. Then, the vowels will fall into a more natural position as an internal stretch replaces the need for external exaggeration.

Exercise 67

Separated /vĭ/ as in Kit

You might wonder how often the "v" sound appears in English, and the answer plenty. What many of us do not realize is that it is the "v" sound ends the word of, a well as a myriad of common vocabulary words in songs like love, move, over, etc. Th "v" belongs to the fricative family, which describes the friction of its articulation. You top front teeth rest on your lower lip and a buzzing friction occurs as you voice th consonant. It, too, has a silent partner, the consonant "f."

Interestingly, when you practice with voiced consonants, you automatically exer cise the unvoiced partner, since the voiced consonant has stronger muscle movemen You essentially get two consonant workouts for the price of one!

1. Breathe to five slowly and silently through your mouth.

2. Press your upper teeth on your lower lip for a moment to initiate the consc nant v.

3. As you pronounce the v, linger on it and create a slight buzz before pronounc ing the vowel.

4. Next, use that buzzing energy to assist your muscles to move into the natura smiley stretch and sing the /ĭ/.

5. Continue to invoke the natural smiley stretch while you sing the /ĭ/.

6. Release the vowel with your breath.

7. Relax your mouth but do not collapse your breath. Simply inhale and prepar for the next syllable.

Audio Track: 67D and 67A

vĭ   vĭ   vĭ   vĭ   vĭ

Exercise 68

Spoken Connected /hmm . . . mĭ_mĭ/

Before singing this exercise, you will speak the connected /mĭ/ sounds. As with the previous exercise, begin with a strong hum, followed by five /mĭ/ syllables. Your lips and facial muscles will move back and forth between the mouth position of the consonant m and the /ĭ/ vowel.

Audio Track: 68S

hmm . . . mĭ_mĭ_mĭ_mĭ_mĭ____

Exercise 69

Sung Connected /hmm . . . mĭ_mĭ /

Sing the following exercise by using the muscle movements you learned in the previous spoken exercise. Remember to smile again on every syllable! This exercise engages the cheek muscles in particular to aid in the development of flexibility and strength in the face. Make sure to add a hum to the first /mĭ/ syllable to reinforce the natural smiley stretch. Sing this five-note-scale exercise slowly in front of a mirror, checking to make sure you are consistently stretching back to the natural smiley stretch position.

Audio Track: 69D and 69A

Exercise 70

Separated /zuh/ as in Strut

The consonant z is great fun to sing, and it does occur frequently at the end of words, especially in the verb is when it precedes a word beginning with a vowel. The z is yet another strong voiced consonant. (Its unvoiced partner consonant is s.)

As you pronounce it, let it buzz for a moment in the same manner as the consonant v in Exercise 67. The /uh/ vowel is one that we barely notice, as it does not have a strong natural mouth movement. In fact, there is hardly any stretchiness at all, which can cause relaxed singing articulation. For that reason, you will practice the /uh/ with a natural smiley stretch in order to wake up this vowel in your mouth!

1. Breathe to five slowly and silently through your mouth.

2. Press your tongue behind your lower teeth for a moment to initiate the consonant /z/.

3. As you pronounce the /z/, linger on it and create a slight buzz before pronouncing the vowel.

4. Next, use that buzzing energy to assist your muscles to move into the natural smiley stretch and sing the /uh/.

5. Continue to invoke the natural smiley stretch while you sing the /uh/.

6. Release the vowel with your breath.

7. Relax your mouth but do not collapse your breath. Simply inhale and prepare for the next syllable.

Audio Track: 70D and 70A

zuh   zuh   zuh   zuh   zuh

<u>Exercise 71</u>

Spoken Connected /hmm . . . muh_muh/

Before singing this exercise, you will speak the connected /muh/ sounds. As with the previous exercise, begin with a strong hum followed by five /muh/ syllables. Your lips and facial muscles will move back and forth between the mouth position of the consonant m and the /uh/ vowel sound.

Audio Track: 71S

hmm . . . muh_muh_muh_muh_muh____

Exercise 72

Sung Connected /hmm . . . muh_muh/

Sing the following exercise by using the muscle movements you learned in the previous spoken exercise. Remember to smile again on every syllable! This exercise engages the cheek muscles in particular to aid in the development of flexibility and strength in the face. Make sure to add a hum to the first /muh/ syllable to reinforce the natural smiley stretch.

Sing this five-note-scale exercise slowly in front of a mirror, checking to make sure you are consistently stretching back to the natural smiley stretch position.

Audio Track: 72D and 72A

THE PRACTICE ROOM

Please remember that the first two tracks, 7D, 18A, and the last, 35D or 35A, are here to warm up and warm down your voice, and you should always include these in your practicing. Your voice teacher of vocal coach may choose to omit one or two tracks if you need a shorter practice session. Be careful not to leave out any track numbers that you learned this week, though. Remember, it is not the quantity of time you practice, but the quality of the muscle movements that create results.

Practice Plans 19A, 19B, and 19C focus on the vowel sounds /ĭ/ and /uh/ as presented in exercises 67-72. Practice Plan 19D includes all stretchy vowels learned thus far in exercises 61-72.

Practice Plan 19A

The /ĭ/ Vowel

As you pronounce the "v," linger on it and create a slight buzz before pronouncing the vowel. The sound may remind you of a cell phone on vibrate. Do not do it too long, as it will cause your lips to tickle, and, as funny as that sounds, it actually is quite

157

uncomfortable. The idea is just to make sure you are working out the consonant posi tion enough to assist with strong articulation.

Practice Plan 19B

The /uh/ Vowel

As you pronounce the /z/, linger on it and create a slight buzz before pronounc ing the vowel. Do not do it too long, as it will cause your tongue to tickle, and, a funny as that sounds, it actually is quite uncomfortable. The idea is just to make sure you are working out the consonant position enough to assist in a strong articulation.

You can use that buzzing energy to assist your muscles to move into the natura smiley stretch and sing the /uh/.

Practice Plan 19C

The /ĭ/ and /uh/ Vowels

Practice Plan 19D

The /ā/, /ah/, /ĭ/, and /uh/ Vowels

Exercise 73

Separated /hmm . . . meh/ as in Dress

This exercise is similar to the ones you have done for the /ee/ vowel. You may sing a slight hum before the m, if that is helpful.

1. Breathe through your mouth to position five.

2. Begin the onset of the vocal sound by closing your mouth and, as you sing the hum, stretch your smiling muscles. Speak the hmm for at least one full beat.

3. Continue voicing the hum but, as you do, relax your lip and cheek muscles.

4. Press your lips together to pronounce the m, and then use the consonant sound m to stretch your muscles into the smiley position to speak the /eh/ vowel This will produce the syllable /hmm . . . meh/.

5. Continue to invoke the natural smiley stretch while you sing the /eh/.

6. Release the vowel with your breath.

7. Relax your mouth but do not collapse your breath. Simply inhale and prepare for the next syllable.

158

Audio Track: 73D and 73A

hmm...meh   meh   meh   meh   meh

Exercise 74

Spoken Connected /hmm . . . meh_meh/

Before singing this exercise, you will speak the connected /meh/ sounds. As with the previous exercise, begin with a strong hum followed by five /meh/ syllables. Your lips and facial muscles will move back and forth between the mouth position of the consonant m and the /eh/ vowel.

Audio Track: 74S

hmm . . . meh_meh_meh_meh_meh_____

Exercise 75

Sung Connected /hmm . . . meh/

Sing the following exercise by using the muscle movements you learned in the previous spoken exercise. Remember to smile again on every syllable! This exercise engages the cheek muscles in particular to aid in the development of flexibility and strength in the face. Make sure to add a hum to the first /meh/ syllable to reinforce the natural smiley stretch.

Sing this five-note-scale exercise slowly in front of a mirror, checking to make sure you are consistently stretching back to the natural smiley stretch position.

Audio Track: 75D and 75A

hmm...meh   meh   meh   meh   meh_____

Exercise 76

Separated /kă/ as in Trap

This exercise is the only one in this set of stretchy vowels that uses an unvoiced consonant. You produce a k at the back of your throat with a light clicking sound. Its voiced consonant, g, is a more difficult consonant choice for a vocal exercise because it closes the throat for a moment. In this instance, practicing the lighter movement of the k is more beneficial for creating flexibility in the articulation, and this active practicing of the k will make your g articulation easier.

The last stretchy vowel is an /ă/ as in trap. This vowel has a tendency to be nasal, and you need to take care to invoke the natural smiley stretch. Another strategy is to think about the position for the /ah/ vowel, which will open up the back a bit by slightly lifting the palate.

1. Breathe to five slowly and silently through your mouth.

2. Pronounce the consonant k.

3. As you pronounce the k, use that energy to assist your cheek muscles to move into the natural smiley stretch to sing the /ă/.

4. Continue to invoke the natural smiley stretch while you sing the /ă/.

5. Release the vowel with your breath.

6. Relax your mouth but do not collapse your breath. Simply inhale and prepare for the next syllable.

Audio Track: 76D and 76A

 kă   kă   kă   kă   kă

Exercise 77

Spoken Connected /hmm . . . mă_mă/

Before singing this exercise, you will speak the connected /mā/ sounds. As with the previous exercise, begin with a strong hum followed by five /mā/ syllables. Your lips and facial muscles will move back and forth between the mouth position of the consonant m and the /ā/ vowel.

Audio Track: 77S

hmm . . . mă_mă_mă_mă_mă____

Exercise 78

Sung Connected /hmm . . . mă___mă /

Sing the following exercise by using the muscle movements you learned in the previous spoken exercise. Remember to smile again on every syllable! This exercise engages the cheek muscles in particular to aid in the development of flexibility and strength in the face. Make sure to add a hum to the first /mă/ syllable to reinforce the natural smiley stretch.

Sing this five-note-scale exercise slowly in front of a mirror, checking to make sure you are consistently stretching back to the natural smiley stretch position.

Audio Track: 78D and 78A

hmm...mă   mă   mă   mă   mă_____

The Practice Room

Please remember that the first two tracks, 7D, 18A, and the last, 35D or 35A, are there to warm up and warm down your voice, and you should always include these in your practicing. Your voice teacher of vocal coach may choose to omit one or two tracks if you need a shorter practice session. Be careful not to leave out any track numbers that you learned this week, though. Remember, it is not the quantity of time you practice, but the quality of the muscle movements that create results.

Practice Plans 20A, 20B, and 20C focus on the vowel sounds /eh/ and /ă/ as presented in exercises 73-78.

Practice Plan 20D includes all stretchy vowels learned thus far in exercises 60-78.

Practice Plan 20A

The /eh/ Vowel

Remember to press your lips together to pronounce the "m," and then use the consonant sound "m" to stretch your muscles into the smiley position to speak the

161

/eh/ vowel. This will produce the syllable /hmm . . . meh/. Continue to invoke the natural smiley stretch while you sing the /eh/.

Practice Plan 20B

The /ă/ Vowel

Remember to press your lips together to pronounce the "m," and then use the consonant sound "m" to stretch your muscles into the smiley position to speak the /ă/ vowel. This will produce the syllable /hmm . . . mă/. Continue to invoke the natural smiley stretch while you sing the /ă/.

Practice Plan 20C

The /eh/ and /ă/ Vowels

Practice Plan 20D

The /ah/, /ā/, /ih/, /uh/, /eh/, and /ă/ Vowels

HELPFUL HINTS

It would be quite a challenge to focus on and study all of the vowels in the English language, especially because it is so rich in variation of pronunciation. The six vowels introduced in this chapter cover general articulation for American English. Practicing all of the vowels presented so far will help you to develop good vocal tone for nine common American English vowel sounds: /oh/, /oo/, /ee/, /ah/, /eh/, /ă/, /ā/, /uh/, and /ĭ/. This will address most of the pronunciation needs you will encounter. Since many of these are building blocks for other vocal sounds, you will have a firm foundation from which to create a consistent vocal tone.

Another reason to limit the study of vowels in this book is so that you will retain your own sound. When singing in other languages, such as French, creating the best sound and accent possible for that language is very important. As we know, American English accents are highly diverse and regional. If we leave a little bit of that accent in your singing, you will be able to sound natural when singing in English. Now, if you are a classical singer, that is a different story, and you will need to work a little more on producing a consistent standard English vowel pronunciation.

ACCESS TO AUDIO TRACKS, VIDEOS AND PRACTICE PLANS

To set up free 12-month online access

1. Visit https://VocalFitnessStudio.com/pbonline

2. Use coupon code DQ$w&Tm%K8P32eb#

Printed in Great Britain
by Amazon

24480846R00099